THE THIRD VIEW OF TONGUES

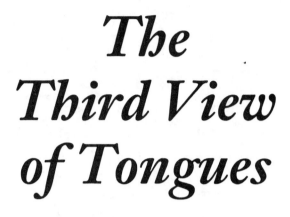

The Third View of Tongues

A surprising and forceful case for the middle ground

K. Neill Foster

HORIZON BOOKS
CAMP HILL, PENNSYLVANIA

Horizon Books
3825 Hartzdale Drive
Camp Hill, PA 17011

ISBN: 0-88965-051-9
© 1994 K. Neill Foster
Originally copyrighted © 1975 by Bethany
Fellowship, Inc., under the title *Help! I Believe in Tongues*
All rights reserved
Printed in the United States of America

94 95 96 97 98 7 6 5 4 3

Cover Design: D Square Design

Preface

Have you ever had the "Help! I believe in tongues" feeling? I certainly have—and for a long time. This book is the result of that kind of feeling. In one sense this dissertation is a *third view* of speaking in tongues. It certainly is not new and probably millions of Christians have held it before me.

But today between the ever louder *yes* and the ever more adamant *no* there is room for a *maybe*. With all of the spiritual gifts, it is "as He wills."

Moreover, with glossolalia surging among historic Christian denominations and in the Roman Catholic church itself, there is a need for spiritual discernment. This manuscript is a contribution toward that need.

My prayer is not that you will see as I do, but only that *agape* love will multiply through these pages. And, that God will grant genuine manifestations of His Holy Spirit in His church.

I am truly grateful that God allowed me first to write *A Revolution of Love* because, not only scripturally but in our lives as well, truths about the gifts of the Holy Spirit need to be set in a context of love.

Some of the statements here are strong. Earlier in my ministry I could not have conceived of strong statements as being related to love at all. But one learns. Charles G. Finney once said, "They greatly err who suppose that benevolence is all softness under all circumstances. Severity is not cruelty but is love manifesting strictness, rigor, and purity when occasion demands."

Thus I have submitted every page to a test of love. Whether or not I have been successful, you may judge for yourself.

K. Neill Foster

Contents

CHAPTER 1

Help! I Believe in Tongues

Right in the middle of a local controversy! That was where my first message landed me.

It was my first time in a certain country, which I should not name at this point, and I had chosen the theme, "Our Three Enemies." I talked about Satan, sin and self. I made clear from my remarks that self was the Christian's formidable enemy and that sin had to be confessed. But I also affirmed the reality of Satan and the possibility of demonic invasion.

The reference to occult subjection was my downfall. One of the area pastors was engaging in a deliverance ministry, and the others were protesting that no such thing as casting out demons should ever be done.

Understandably enough, my hosts were somewhat alarmed. One leader said to me, "You didn't really mean what you said; we know what you meant." And, still naive and unaware of the local controversy, I blundered on. "Oh yes," I said, referring to my illustration, "we really saw a case of demon possession."

The persecuted pastor, on the other hand, stuck to me like a burr—and that was understandable. I had unwittingly identified myself with him in his difficulty.

In conversing with the young pastor later, I found him to be hurting but sane, even loving those who disagreed with him.

Then, while I went with the mission leader to the interior of the country, a special convention was held by a minister of another denomination in the young pastor's church, and forty or fifty of the Latin believers there spoke in tongues. Their excitement knew no bounds.

And my consternation increased. On the one side I was under pressure to denounce the tongues-speakers. And in my heart I wanted nothing to do with opposing anything the Holy Spirit might be doing. When I refused to denounce the young people who were speaking in tongues, the tension increased and the young people flocked to my side.

My two-week ministry went poorly. I was effectively "turned off" by leaders who wanted a repudiation of tongues. I felt like Jeremiah. I was a man with a message, but no one would listen.

On the other side of the coin, I also knew what it was to suffer deep personal loss and the alienation of an honored brother in Christ when he was carried away by the charismatic movement.

In isolated circumstances, apart from regular fellowship with other Christians, a beloved brother in Christ, along with his wife, became involved in a prophecy and gift movement which would certainly be repudiated as left wing and radical by mainline Pentecostal denominations as well as by evangelicals generally.

While I wait for my friend to retrace his steps, while I yearn for a renewal of the loving relationship we once enjoyed, the pain is real. It is as real as the anguish I felt when the pressure was on to denounce the youthful tongues-speakers.

Am I alone between the poles? I think not. And, it seems to me that the charismatic movement hardly needs enemies when events like these buffet its friends.

CHAPTER 2

Charismatic War

Today in Christendom there is war over the charismata. The weapons are not physical but carnal. The instruments of war are words and ideas. The casualties do not bleed, but they are wounded all the same. Finally, that mystical church, which is the body of Christ worldwide, suffers most. The warring factions are easily identified, though these people may have attended the same church for years and, indeed, may look alike and be related in the flesh.

The positions are rigid and well fortified. On the one hand, there are those who say that tongues have ceased. And by their assured logic it is certainly clear to them that speaking in tongues has ceased. The sign gifts of the Holy Spirit are not for today. The supernatural is no longer needed. Instead, great care must be taken to "rightly divide the word of truth." Certainly every word of the Bible is true and verbally inspired. But it should be understood that we today live in another dispensation.

The opposing army has its position, too. After

you are converted to Christ you must certainly experience the "baptism of the Holy Ghost." The evidence of this experience is "speaking in tongues." Everyone may speak in tongues; everyone may have all the gifts of the Holy Spirit. And those who disagree, along with those who are uninitiated, are both cold and unspiritual.

The collision between these two forces of evangelicalism is both loud and painful. Recently I heard the controversy described this way: One group of God's people is in the ditch on one side of the narrow way. And the other group is in the ditch on the other side. They are shouting back and forth across the narrow way at each other, "Our ditch is the best ditch!" To fully document the argument is wholly possible, but not especially necessary.

As one brother has said, "There is a wheelbarrow full of literature on the subject." But what I will do is supply excerpts from a book on each side.

I should make clear that these authors do not reflect any rancor or bitterness in the expressions of their views. The books are well written, without emotional overtones.

New Testament Teaching on Tongues, by Merril F. Unger, pretty well enunciates the fundamentalist, dispensational view. On the charismatic side I have chosen *The Holy Spirit and You* by Dennis and Rita Bennett.

The no-tongues view excerpted from a number of pages is set forth by Dr. Unger as follows:

> Tongues at Pentecost were a witness to events inaugurating a new age.
> Tongues at Pentecost bore no direct relation to the baptism of the Spirit.

What occurred in Acts 2 can be interpreted as a second experience after salvation only if the introductory nature of Pentecost as the inauguration of a new age is completely overlooked.

What occurred in Acts 2 can be construed as a second experience after salvation only if Pentecost is interpreted apart from the total testimony of Scripture, especially the great doctrinal Epistles of the New Testament.

What occurred in Acts 2 can be construed as a second experience after salvation only if an intrinsic and inseparable element of salvation is severed from its place and made something in addition to that salvation.

What occurred in Acts 2 can be construed as a second experience after salvation only if terms that radically differ in meaning are confused and used to denote the same thing.

The temporary character of speaking in tongues is suggested by the mention of it only in very early lists in an early Epistle.

The temporary character of speaking in tongues is also suggested by its inferiority to other gifts in the matter of usefulness.

The temporary character of speaking in tongues is definitely declared by the apostle in contrast to the other gifts in the matter of usefulness.

The temporary character of speaking in tongues is definitely declared by the apostle in contrast to the permanency of love (1 Corinthians 13:1-8).

Tongues were to cease because, in contrast to ever enduring love, they often fail (1 Corinthians 13:8).

Tongues were to cease because, like prophecy and knowledge, they were to be replaced by something better (1 Corinthians 13:8).

Tongues were to cease because, like prophecy and knowledge, they belong to a period of partial revelation before there were any New Testament books in general circulation (1 Corinthians 13:9, 10).

Tongues were to cease because the completed revelation of Scripture in the canonical books of the New Testament would eventually make prophecy, knowledge, and tongues unnecessary and useless (1 Corinthians 13:11, 12).

Speaking in tongues in its temporary character was limited to the apostolic church.[1]

The pro-tongues view, excerpted from several pages, is also clear enough.

You don't have to speak in tongues to have times of feeling filled with the Holy Spirit, but if you want the free and full outpouring that is the baptism in the Holy Spirit, you must expect it to happen as in the Scripture, and to do what Peter, James, John, Paul, Mary, Mary Magdalene, Barnabas, and all the rest did!

"But that would just be me speaking!" Exactly! God does not speak in tongues—people speak in tongues, as the Spirit gives the words. On the day of Pentecost we read: "They began to speak—in other languages—as the Spirit gave them utterance." So you must begin to speak, in other languages—not your own language or languages—as the Spirit gives the utterance, or the form of the words, to you—and He will! Just like a child learning to talk for the first time, open your mouth and speak out the first syllables and expressions that come to your lips. You must begin to speak just as Peter had to get out of the boat. God will guide you when you dare to trust Him by stepping out in faith.

We are convinced, from the Scriptures and after praying with thousands of people to receive the baptism in the Holy Spirit over the past ten years and more, that there is no believer who cannot speak in tongues, if he or she is properly prepared, and really ready to trust the Lord.

However, after the fullness and overflow of the Spirit, any or all nine gifts may be manifested frequently and in power through the life of the believer.

Though all baptized-in-the-Holy-Spirit believers can and should speak in tongues daily in their prayers, not all will minister the gift of tongues in a public meeting (1 Corinthians 12:30).[2]

In these two books not only are the views clearly set forth, but the intense feelings of those who adhere to these views are also evident. Perhaps the most controversial and emotional subject that evangelicals can discuss these days is that of speaking in tongues.

However, you may still ask, why take the time even to partially document such views when you don't agree wholly with either of them?

I intend to set the stage for what I call the "third view of tongues."

CHAPTER 3

The Experience Books

In the last decade a whole corps of new writers has emerged who, having added eloquence to charisma, have done a masterful job of describing the experience of speaking in tongues.

But the books produce a certain uneasiness too. For example, I toyed with various titles for this chapter such as The Experience Books —True, but Not Honest. But I discarded that because it seemed to impugn my brethren (for they are dear brothers) who have written the experience books. For the same reason I rejected another title also, The Experience Books— True but Not Fair. Eventually I decided that it would have to be The Experience Books—True but Not Complete. However, that's too cumbersome. So I'll settle for the title as it now appears.

Now, what am I trying to get at? Here it is as plainly as I can put it. I have no real reason, for example, to doubt what Pat Boone, or John Sherrill or Frances Gardner Hunter have written. The narrative of the tongues ex-

18

perience which they present is credible. This
is what they say.

First, Pat Boone:

> The moment had come. George and I were
> alone in the room. We raised our arms to God,
> and I prayed. "O Father, this is it—I give up.
> I yield my life to You. Please take it, Lord,
> and make of it whatever You want to. Forgive
> me of every sin, wash me clean; and Jesus,
> Oh, precious Jesus, be my baptizer. Baptize me
> right now in Your Spirit, the Spirit of the liv-
> ing God."
>
> Even as I prayed I began to sense the Lord's
> presence in a remarkable way. I began by sim-
> ply offering my voice to Jesus and supporting
> a tone. As I did, a beautiful melody came out,
> and words began to float in on the melody! It
> was such a graceful and beautiful thing that
> I hardly recognized the voice as mine. And the
> warmth and assurance filled my spirit.
>
> How can I describe such a thing? It was an
> uplifting, inspiring, joyful experience—the most
> profound of my life. I had a deep sense of know-
> ing that I was singing a new song to God.[1]

Now I wish to quote from reporter John Sherrill's book, *They Speak with Other Tongues*. Mr.
Sherrill first quotes the words of a Christian
woman:

> What's the use of speaking in tongues? The
> only way I can answer that is to say, "What's
> the use of a bluebird? What is the use of a
> sunset?" Just sheer, unmitigated uplift, just
> joy unspeakable and with it health and peace
> and rest and release from burdens and ten-
> sions.[2]

John Sherrill also relates his own experience:

The group moved closer around me. It was almost as if they were forming with their bodies a funnel through which was concentrated the flow of the Spirit that was pulsing through that room. It flowed into me as I sat there, listening to the Spirit-song around me. Now the tongues swelled to a crescendo, musical and lovely. I opened my mouth, wondering if I too could join in, but nothing happened.

I felt a numbness in my lips and a constriction in my throat.

And suddenly I had the impression that in order to speak in tongues I had only to look up. But this was a joyful gesture. All my training and inclination was to approach God with head bowed.

Strange that such a simple gesture as lifting the head should become a battleground. And soon—perhaps because I did not obey quick enough—another directive came clear; not only was I to lift my head but I was to lift my hands too, and I was to cry out with all the feeling in me a great shout of praise to God. A hot, angry flush rose and flooded me. It was the thing above all things that I didn't want to do.

Perhaps because it was so very repugnant to me the issue was clearly drawn as one of sheer obedience.

What other possible significance could there be in my raising my hands high and mouthing some words of praise? But that was what I had to do, and I knew it. Foolish as it seemed. Or maybe because it seemed foolish. I heard E. Stanley Jones saying, "I had to become God's fool."

With a sudden burst of will I thrust my hands into the air, turned my face full upward, and at the top of my voice I shouted:

"Praise the Lord!"

It was the floodgate opened. From deep inside me, deeper than I knew voice could go, came a torrent of joyful sound. It was not beautiful, like the tongues around me. I had the impression that it was ugly: explosive and grunting. I didn't care. It was healing, it was forgiveness, it was love too deep for words and it burst from me in wordless sound. After that one shattering effort of will, my will was released, freed to soar into union with Him. No further conscious effort was required of me at all, not even choosing the syllables with which to express my joy. The syllables were all there, ready-formed for my use, more abundant than my earth-bound lips and tongue could give shape to.

It was not that I felt out of control of the situation: I had never felt more truly master of myself, more integrated and at peace with warring factions inside myself. I could stop the tongues at any instant, but who would? I wanted them never to stop.

And so I prayed on, laughing and free, while the setting sun shone through the window, and the stars came out.[3]

Finally, I quote from the best-selling author Frances Gardner Hunter:

There was no one in the room but Jesus and me, but the power and the presence of God was as real as it had ever been in my life. I softly whispered a very simple little prayer, "God, if it's genuine, if it's real, if it's of you, and it's for me, then make the water hard, or in my case, make the air solid under the sound of my voice, and Jesus, I ask you to baptize me with the Holy Spirit."

In that moment of yielding to God of my mind, my soul, my spirit, my tongue, my brain, I gave just one or two little sounds, and instantly I was baptized with the Holy Spirit. The room was filled with the most beautiful glow you could ever imagine. I had to close my eyes! The splendor of the Lord was there! The entire room seemed bathed with the love of God. I thought surely I must be in heaven. Never have I felt such a helplessness before God as I did in that moment of yielding. Gone were the barriers I had built up ever since I became a Christian about the matter of praying in tongues. Out of my own mouth flowed the most beautiful, soft "love" language in the world. I knew I was praising and loving God just like the 120 did on the day of Pentecost.

I have never felt closer to God, more loved by God, more protected by Him, more sheltered by Him, or more full of love and praise for Him then in those moments. My cup was running over! I couldn't understand a word I was saying, but I knew God could. My heart knew that in my overflowing with love for the One who had so changed my life, I was praising His Holy Name, and I wasn't cluttering up the praise with some of my own inadequate words, but was using the special "love" language which He had given to me. Jesus speaking of this had said, "Out of your innermost being shall flow rivers of living water." [4]

I find the accounts fascinating. But what is left unsaid? Why is the message, as I suggested earlier, incomplete?

Experience alone within Christianity is not an adequate base for conviction and doctrine. The experience books are probably true. These things happened. And we should not be so sour as to refuse to praise God for everything He has done, if indeed the experiences have been from Him.

It is never spelled out in words, but the experience books generally leave the impression that speaking in tongues is the key to the fullness of the Holy Spirit.

We must also admit that experience is a very important factor in Christianity. "Once I was blind, but now I see." It is hard to argue with it. Facts are facts, you know.

But there is a dangerous lack of balance. Other experiences need to be placed alongside the experience books. In fact, this book is in a way an experience book too.

Other entertainers like Pat Boone have had a revolutionary encounter with Christ apart from the phenomenon of speaking in tongues. Authors like John Sherrill have found abundant life in Christ apart from glossolalia.

New converts such as Frances Hunter have come into the experience of the fullness of the Holy Spirit and great fruitfulness apart from the charismatic movement.

The Experience Books are injurious in that they do not say these things.

Worse, there are other equally reliable and sincere Christian people who can recount cases where demonic tongues have had to be cast out. And if we are in the realm of experience, it is possible to find instances of genuine tongues in the life of a person who remains subjected to the occult. Personally, I know of two such cases. (For a discussion of the question, can a Christian be controlled by a demon?, see Appendix A.)

Experience, then, is a shaky base upon which to build doctrine. And though I have seen an undeniably divine tongue functioning in a demonized person, that is not a proper basis for declaring that tongues cannot be the proof of the fullness of the Holy Spirit. If I say at all that tongues is not the only evidence of the fullness of the Holy Spirit that conviction must be based upon the Word of God. Experiences which do not confirm the Word of God must be questioned. And certainly no experience with supernatural manifestations should ever be made a base for doctrine.

A general observation, which has exceptions of course, is that the less grounded on the Bible a group or an individual may be, the more easily the charismatic movement penetrates. The mainline churches which have reduced their view of the Scriptures, the Roman Catholics who elevate tradition to the level of Scripture, and immature Christians who have not received an extensive knowledge of the Bible all respond readily to an experiential approach.

But in these pages our final and only court of appeal must be the Scriptures, which I take to be inerrant and verbally inspired as originally given. If the Bible will support the position taken, fine. But if it does not support a given position, then the view needs to be changed. Lacking a wide biblical base, an experience book can be harmful, even destructive. In my view the experience books have been harmful because of what has been left unsaid and what is implied.

CHAPTER 4

The Case for More

Is there a God-ordained experience that may take place in the life of the believer that can be recognized as an experience subsequent to the conversion experience?

This question must be answered because it has a direct bearing upon spiritual gifts. In the book of Acts, especially, the manifestation of spiritual gifts seems to accompany an experience that happens to new Christians.

Some of you will disagree with me here. But please hear me out. I have some important things to share as the teaching of this book unfolds.

Pentecost, with the initial manifestation of speaking in other languages, was an experience for the disciples. But since the outpouring of the Spirit marked the beginning of the church, it would be difficult to say that Acts 2 in itself substantiates the teaching of a "second blessing."

Further on in Acts, in my view, it becomes quite clear that there was indeed something that happened to Christians, an experience subsequent to conversion.

Samaritan experience

In Acts 8 we have the Samaritan account of individuals being filled with the Spirit (vv. 5-15). Many had been converted and baptized through the ministry of Philip. But the disciples at Jerusalem, upon hearing that the Samaritans received the word of God, sent Peter and John down to pray for them. If we can judge by Philip's treatment of the Ethiopian later in the same chapter, he was not in the habit of baptizing people unless they were believers. The Samaritans had believed, were converted, and were Christians. They also had been baptized in water. But still they lacked, so the disciples went to pray for them with the laying on of hands. And the Samaritans received the Holy Spirit.

To suggest they were not saved until they received the Holy Spirit is to admit at the same time that they were baptized in water before they were converted. Evangelicals today certainly would not countenance that.

It is a fair conclusion that the principle "unto him that hath it shall be given" was functioning. New believers, born of the Spirit, baptized in water, then received the fullness of the Holy Spirit. The implications to Christians who have been converted and who have followed the Lord in baptism are considerable. God has something more.

Paul's experience

In chapter 9 of Acts Saul's conversion on the Damascus road is related. It was as dramatic a conversion as anyone could have: a bright light, a voice, and a trembling pursuer of Christians falls to the ground. He is left blinded. Spectacular indeed!

But after three days Ananias was sent to pray for Saul that he might receive his sight and be filled with the Holy Spirit. Assuming that Paul was then filled with the Holy Spirit, there was an interval of three days between his surrender to Christ and the enduement of the Holy Spirit.

Without straining at anything it appears that Paul's experience was similar to that of the Samaritans'.

We should also note at this point that no specific mention of speaking in tongues has been made in these two cases. Simon the sorcerer certainly did observe something that made him illicitly covet the authority to lay on hands, but to insist that the Samaritans spoke in tongues is to go beyond what the Scripture says. Also there is no suggestion that Paul spoke in tongues when he was filled with the Holy Spirit, though of course he ultimately received the gift (1 Cor. 14:18).

Cornelius' experience

In Acts 10 we have the unique story of Cornelius. He was a military man of influence with a hundred men under his command. He was devout, God-fearing, a man who gave alms and was always praying.

There was at least one devout soldier who served under him. The reputation of Cornelius was unusual. As a member of an occupation army, he was held in high esteem by the Jews as righteous and God-fearing. And what conquered nation has ever loved the occupation army?

Still Cornelius was not a saved man, though his prayers were being answered and his giving noted (v. 4). This is clear from chapter 11, verse 14. Peter was to be received because he would deliver "words by which you shall be saved." And Cornelius received Peter.

If ever there was a man ready to receive the gospel it was Cornelius. And while Peter preached, the Spirit fell on his whole family. The manifestation was dual—speaking in tongues and magnifying God.

What happened? Two things at least. Cornelius was converted and he was filled with the Holy Spirit. Both things happened together, but if you wish to separate split-second blessings, you may say that he was converted and filled with the Spirit, not filled with the Spirit and converted. Peter appears to be astounded because the Gentiles received the same gift the Jews had received earlier.

Jesus talked about the Spirit of truth whom the world could not receive (John 14:17). If not the world, then who? The church of course. The believers. The fullness of the Holy Spirit is the believers' experience.

Cornelius' experience presents the possibility of a simultaneous conversion and Spirit-filled experience. It also presents the possibility, though not the necessity, of speaking in tongues as a manifestation of the Spirit's fullness.

The Ephesians' experience

In Acts 19:1-7 we have a fascinating account of Paul's encounter with twelve men who evidently, somehow, had been left out of the main-stream of the dynamic events in the early church.

They had received John's baptism, which was a baptism of repentance.

But Paul questioned them closely, "Have you received the Holy Spirit since [or when] you believed?"

Their answer demonstrated their isolation. "We have not so much as heard whether there be any Holy Spirit."

And what does Paul do? Does he then lay hands on them that they might receive the Holy Spirit? Not at all.

Instead, he baptized them in water. And I seriously doubt that Paul would baptize un-converted people. These, then, were new con-verts, perhaps led to Christ by Paul himself then and there. (And for some concerned souls, here is a scriptural warrant for being baptized twice if the first baptism took place before saving faith dawned.)

These Ephesians, certainly saved, baptized as well, now receive the laying on of hands from Paul. And they speak in tongues and prophesy.

The key again, as in the Samaritan passage, is on the point of baptism. It really does not matter if one translates Paul's question "since" or "when." According to Paul's conversation with them, they were obviously saved people who were then baptized in Jesus' name and sub-sequently filled with the Holy Spirit.

The implication again is consistent with the other passages already considered. There is something more for believers.

The terms used vary: "Received the Holy Spirit," "filled with the Holy Spirit." In predicting the Pentecost experience Jesus said the disciples would be "baptized with the Holy Spirit."

Terminology, it seems to me, is of minor importance here, especially since the Bible uses various terms. What is important is that we experience what God has for us.

The danger in reviewing these passages is to go farther than the Holy Spirit goes. The scriptures we have just considered clearly demonstrate a second experience for the believer. But they stop short of insisting that speaking in tongues is the only, or even necessary, evidence of being filled with the Holy Spirit.

I find Larry Christenson's comment helpful at this point:

> Is speaking in tongues the only objective manifestation that a person has had this definite, instantaneous experience of the baptism with the Holy Spirit? Scripture does not say that it is the only one. . . . In two cases in the Book of Acts the objective manifestation is not mentioned; in three it is, and in all of these the manifestation is speaking in tongues.
>
> This is as far as we can go theologically. We can discern the pattern of the baptism with the Holy Spirit in the Book of Acts, and see the part which speaking in tongues plays in it. But we cannot set this down as a rigid doctrine or formula. Scripture itself shows us that the pattern allows for considerable flexibility.[1]

And essentially this is the third view of tongues: God divides the spiritual gifts severally as He wills. Sometimes when people are filled with the Holy Spirit they speak in tongues. Many times they do not. The important thing is to be filled with the Holy Spirit—and know it.

Speaking in a context relating to the coming of the Comforter, Jesus said, "At that day ye shall *know* . . . I will . . . manifest myself unto you" (John 14:20, 21). Jesus did not tell His disciples what the manifestation would be or how they would know, only that they would know and that He would manifest himself to them.

And surely every Christian has the right and the need to know for certain that he has been filled with the Holy Spirit.

> In the documentary film, *Eastward to Asia*, issued by the Billy Graham Evangelistic Association, Dr. Graham is seen at one point addressing several thousand Indian Christian workers. The subject of his early morning address is "Be Filled with the Spirit."
>
> In his own inimitable way Dr. Graham asks these questions: "Are you filled with the Spirit? Do you know it? Do you know it?"
>
> We turn these questions to those of you who read these lines. Are *you* filled with the Spirit? Do you *know* it?
>
> "Wherefore be ye not unwise, but understanding what the will of the Lord is. And be not drunk with wine, wherein is excess; but be filled with the Spirit" (Eph. 5:17-18).[2]

CHAPTER 5

Gifts for Today

The Nine Gifts of the Spirit Are Not for Today. That is the title of a book in my library which I have read but with which I cannot agree. I must go on to say that the author would certainly be classed as evangelical, if not a fundamentalist.

As I have documented in a previous chapter there is the view that "tongues have ceased." It is imperative in this discussion of the "third view" to face this issue. I believe that the gifts of the Holy Spirit are for today for the following reasons:

1. The spiritual gifts were an integral part of the operation of the New Testament church. "God also bearing them witness, both with signs and wonders, and with divers miracles, and gifts of the Holy Ghost, according to his own will" (Heb. 2:4).

2. When the Holy Spirit was poured out in New Testament times, the manifestation of a spiritual gift followed (Acts 2:4; 8:17; 10:46; 19:6).

3. There is no scripture to suggest that spiritual gifts have ceased, although some endeavor to support such a cause with a questionable interpretation of 1 Corinthians 13:8.

4. An examination of 1 Corinthians 13:8 also demonstrates that the spiritual gifts shall one day cease, but it cannot be proved that this has already come to pass. If we say tongues have ceased, we must also, to be consistent, affirm that knowledge and prophecy have passed away. If Paul is referring in 1 Corinthians 13:8 to secular knowledge, we have only to remind ourselves that scientists now discuss the "knowledge explosion."

If Paul is here referring to the word of knowledge as a spiritual gift, then obviously abilities such as Peter demonstrated in his dealing with Ananias and Sapphira are still in the church today. To what or whom must these abilities be attributed if the gift of the word of knowledge is nonexistent today? To label all manifestations as soulish or diabolical is faulty logic and dangerous as well. Is not the unpardonable sin attributing the work of the Holy Spirit to Satan?

And what shall we say of prophecies? Have they failed? Hardly. Many which refer especially to Israel are in the process of fulfillment. If the sign gifts are only for Israel, since 1948 the Jews have been back in the ball game. If Paul is here referring to inspired preaching, there is probably not an evangelical anywhere who would say that the day of preaching is past— not in a world which is responsive to the gospel as never before.

If Paul is here speaking about the prophetic utterance, the most recent and most widely publicized prophecy was that of Duncan Campbell, esteemed Presbyterian revivalist who announced beforehand that revival would come to Canada and that it would begin in the Ebenezer Baptist Church in Saskatoon. And the record stands. One of the most unusual visitations of the Holy Spirit in Canadian history did begin there in 1971.

No, it is not possible to say honestly that tongues have ceased unless it is admitted that knowledge and prophecy have also terminated. To do that is to ignore scriptural truth and present experience.

5. In 1 Corinthians 13:10 Paul talks about that which is "perfect" coming to do away with the gifts in question. Many say today that the perfect is the Word of God. And while God's Word is perfect, the tip-off, it seems to me, comes in the phrase "face to face" (v. 12). It is an obvious reference to the coming of Jesus Christ to establish His kingdom. And, we should agree, Paul is saying that when the Saviour returns, when we see Him face to face, these gifts will cease—but not before.

The gifts of the Holy Spirit were in the church yesterday. And I believe they are still present today. Thank God.

CHAPTER 6

Gifts Don't Make
You Spiritual

Before launching into a study and description
of the spiritual gifts and this view of speaking
in tongues, there is a need to set out basic principles relating to the charismata.

First, the gifts of the Holy Spirit are for all
Christians. God has divided to "every man, severally as he wills" (1 Cor. 12:7.) Not a single
Christian believer has been left out. There are
some who believe that these spiritual gifts come
to every Christian at conversion and are in the
life in seed form until the person experiences
the fullness of the Holy Spirit. And this would
be in keeping with the scriptural principle—
Jericho was given into Joshua's hands, but he
still had to possess it.

Another vital principle which may cause
some shock waves is this: God's gifts and call-
ings are "without repentance" (Rom. 11:29).
While the context does indeed relate to Israel,
the word used for gift in the original language
is *charismata*.

In this connection I want to point out that those who spoke with tongues in Acts *began to do so* and *continued to do so.*

T. J. McCrossan makes this point very well. In his book on this subject[1] he points out that in each of the three cases where tongues are mentioned in the book of Acts (2:4; 10:44-46; 19:6) the coming of the Holy Spirit upon the individuals involved is in the aorist Greek tense. For the layman, this means that something definitely happened at a specific point in time and it was completed at that point—a definite completed act in the past.

Mr. McCrossan goes on to observe that in each of the three passages the verbs used to describe speaking in tongues are all imperfect tense, not aorist. That means that the act was something which occurred in the past and then *continued to keep happening.*

The coming of the Holy Spirit in the tongues passages was clear-cut and precise in a point of time. The tongues experience, on the other hand, was something that happened and kept on happening—a continuous experience.

And the point the author makes is that the tongues experience in Acts was the gift of tongues which continued to be manifested and that there is no serious way that the Acts experiences can be made to be a "baptism of the Holy Spirit" with the initial evidence of speaking in tongues as distinct from the gift of tongues which is later described in First Corinthians, chapter twelve.

An illustration of this imperfect tense occurs in Mark 5:8 on another subject. Our English Bibles generally say something like this, "Jesus said, Come out of him, you unclean spirit."

But the Amplified New Testament makes clear, as does the Spanish with which I am personally familiar, "Jesus *kept saying,* Come out of him, you unclean spirit." In the liberation of persons from occult bondage, repetitious commanding is many times, though not always, necessary.

This teaching on the imperfect tense repudiates the teaching that the sign of the baptism with the Holy Spirit is one thing, and the gift of speaking in tongues is another. Not only is it impossible to substantiate such teaching scripturally, but the Bible also teaches the opposite: those who speak in tongues continue to do so. Many times I have counselled tongues-speakers along this line. The gifts are permanent.

Again, the gifts because of their very permanence cannot be made to be signs of spirituality. In both the Old Testament and the New it can be demonstrated that spiritual gifts do not make a person spiritual. Take for example Balaam, the prophet. Every time he opened his mouth to prophesy he blessed Israel. His prophecies were flawless because they were obviously prompted of God. But he owned a rebel heart. Though he could not and did not curse Israel, he did pass the word on the side to Balak that the way to destroy Israel was to suck them into idolatry and sensuality.

In the New Testament the Corinthians came "behind in no spiritual gift" (1 Cor. 1:7). They had them all. But Paul makes clear that they were still carnal—charismatic but carnal. That was the view from Corinth.

Psalm 68:18 has a very interesting and revealing comment: "Thou hast ascended on high, thou hast led captivity captive: thou hast received gifts for men; yea, *for the rebellious also, that the Lord God might dwell among them.*"

Though it is interesting that Paul's New Testament quotation of this verse in Ephesians 4 omits any reference to the rebellious receiving gifts, the implication is there. And the possibility that rebellious people might indeed have spiritual gifts is present. The point we are making here is that spiritual gifts do not make one spiritual. The Holy Spirit does that.

Contemporary experience also confirms that spiritual gifts are not signs of spirituality. A preacher who was involved in a sordid affair with another woman defended himself before his wife, saying, "What I'm doing can't be wrong. People are finding the Lord when I preach." And so they were. But he had failed to distinguish between a spiritual gift and spirituality.

In a city in the plains of Colombia I was asked to preach an evangelistic campaign. The meetings proved especially difficult, and one of the reasons was that the last evangelist who had conducted meetings there had been disorderly, deceitful, and treacherous, though beyond doubt, charismatic. People had come as early as 3 o'clock in the afternoon seeking the miracles that were occurring in his meetings. But the evangelist was under discipline from his own respected denomination in Peru. Instead of submitting to correction and discipline, he simply moved his operations to Colombia. Toward the end of his campaign the local pastors had to go to him and rebuke him to his face for his unethical practices.

That such examples might be multiplied endlessly does not negate the possibility or the reality of spiritual gifts. It simple demonstrates what I said earlier: spiritual gifts have no clear connection to spirituality or Christ-adorning behavior. If they are genuine gifts, they are received from the Lord in a spiritual experience. There are many who have begun in the Spirit but have ended in the flesh—gifts operating all the while.

A youthful companion and friend in the ministry experienced the gift of tongues. Years later he was about to repudiate it as invalid. His reasoning was, "I doubted the tongues because I was able to exercise it and live in sin at the same time."

Because of the prevailing attitude toward tongues not too many charismatics confront this issue, but Don Basham is one who does.

> We have mistakenly assumed the gifts of the Spirit were an endorsement of character.
>
> Although people tend to accept the gifts of the Spirit as the mark of the true or false apostle or prophet, the word of God insists it is Christ-like character, not the miraculous gifts, which determine His status.
>
> God gives and doesn't take back.
>
> "For the gifts and the call of God are irrevocable" (Romans 11:29, RSV).

This scripture verse offers another explanation for the existence of the false prophet who manifests genuine gifts. The word "gifts" used in this verse is the word charismata, the same word Paul uses to describe spiritual gifts in First Corinthians 12. So Paul implies that God gives spiritual gifts to men and no matter what sin a man may fall into, God does not revoke His gifts. Here we have a conflict between what man thinks God should do and what God chooses to do. The understandable human reaction is, "If I were God, I wouldn't do it that way. If I gave a miraculous ministry to a man and he fell into sin, I'd take the power away."

That's the human way, all right: pour out the miracles as long as the man behaves himself, but snatch them away the moment he steps out of line. But that is not God's way.

"For my thoughts are not your thoughts, neither are your ways my ways, saith the Lord. For as the heavens are higher than the earth, so are my ways higher than your ways, and my thoughts than your thoughts" (Isaiah 55:8-9, KJV).

Our responsibility is not to try to change God's methods but to understand His ways and flow with them. We need to say with David:

"Shew me thy ways, O Lord; teach me thy paths. Lead me in thy truth, and teach me: for thou art the God of my salvation; . . . " (Psalm 25:4-5, KJV).

But since the gifts of the Holy Spirit are not given because a man behaves properly, neither are they removed because a man behaves improperly! [2]

A word of caution here. A good man does not necessarily have good doctrine. The most dangerous of false prophets is one who has excellent character—and diabolical doctrine: Paul repeatedly urged Timothy to watch doctrine (1 Tim. 4).

Why God sovereignly bestows His gifts without repentance I cannot say. But Satan knows well how to take advantage of divine order. And as long as Christians make spiritual gifts marks of spirituality they fall into enemy hands. Of the false prophets Jesus repeatedly said, "By their fruits ye shall know them."

Let's consider another principle: God divides severally as He wills. God's gifts are given plurally, in His will (1 Cor. 12:7, 11). This charismatic plurality opens up a wide vista which beckons the believer. Through all his Christian experience he can be and should be coveting the best gifts, remembering always that plurality is in God's will.

I must interject here that just because God divides the gifts as He wills, we need not be paralyzed in our prayers. He can and often does reveal His will concerning specific spiritual gifts. "Covet earnestly" is a strong term in the original language.

But, and this is yet another principle relating to spiritual gifts, the spiritual gifts are not to be demanded. God divides "severally as he wills." To demand what may not be God's will draws the believer off the security of biblical ground and allows the enemy to substitute the false and demonic.

And let there be no doubt that this happens especially with the gift of tongues, which many tend to demand.

It is often claimed that if one covers himself with the blood of Jesus Christ, there is no danger of deception or the demonic.

But in practical experience a fairly large percentage of charismatic seekers get into difficulty right there.

Why? I, for one, stoutly believe in the protection and efficacy of Jesus' incorruptible blood *now*. In spiritual warfare on numerous occasions I have claimed and appreciated the present power of the blood of Christ.

But, we would agree, a man could not go out and commit adultery and avoid entanglement with Satan while he committed adultery because he was claiming the protection of Jesus' blood. Adultery has to be off-limits, off biblical ground.

In Moses' time the Israelis in Egypt were protected by the blood on the doorposts. Only the homes of the Jews were protected. Had an Israeli firstborn son ventured out that dark night, he would surely have died.

The analogy is clear. Christians who forsake biblical ground to seek experiences out of God's will are vulnerable. And all too frequently, they are the helpless victims of Satan—because they have foolishly forsaken biblical ground to demand a certain charismatic manifestation. Jesus' blood has lost *none* of its power. But it is not an indiscriminate cover for all kinds of strange and eccentric behavior.

In passing I have already emphasized that the spiritual gifts are to be coveted earnestly. When we get down to business it is not long till God meets us. The first step in seeking spiritual gifts is always to submit to God's will (1 Cor. 12:11; Heb. 2:4). Once God's will is clear regarding a certain gift, seek with all your heart; you will not be disappointed.

Still another principle: Prophecy is the most desirable gift. Today we live in an evangelical era reluctantly engrossed with the gift of tongues. And I cannot escape this atmosphere, as you have noted by the title of this book.

Imagine what the situation might be around the world if the charismatic emphasis in the church of Jesus Christ focused on inspired preaching. We are especially to desire to prophesy (1 Cor. 14:5). Instead, to our detriment and the enemy's advantage, we are often warring over tongues.

Now a final principle: Not all speak with tongues. We might as easily say that not all are apostles, but not all are seeking to be apostles. Unfortunately, in many situations, all are seeking to speak in tongues. And the Scriptures clearly point to the contrary. In 1 Corinthians 12:29, 30 the answer to each question is presumed to be *no*. At least that is what the English suggests. But the Greek is stronger. Preceding each of the questions in the original language is the Greek negative *mē*. The only possible answer is *no*. Not all are apostles and not all speak in tongues. The series of negatives is especially important when tongues are mentioned because that is where the church is hurting today.

Personally, I feel that to say not all will speak with tongues "in the church" is to evade what Paul is saying here. In verse 27, Paul appears to be referring to the body of Christ, not just to the Corinthian assembly or to a church meeting.

And if the "in the church" emphasis circumnavigates a plain statement of scripture, could it not in some cases blow a hole in the protective dike Paul's teaching seeks to place around Christ's church?

The seeking after tongues also is contrary to the divine exhortation to seek His face (Ps. 27:8). Instead of the head we are absorbed with the hand. Distorted seeking can only beget strange finding. Surely we should seek the Giver, not the gifts!

To insist or imply all must or could speak in tongues is to disfigure the body. There are six places in the New Testament where Paul lists spiritual abilities. In each case there is a context relating to the body of Christ. To magnify one gift is like having a nose a yard long, or an ear draping on the ground. It is wrong to caricature the body of Christ. Each gift in its place fits into the body. And not all the members are the same. Every cell in the body is a microcosm of the whole, but when one cell seeks to be everything, that is cancer.

One other important point I wish to make. It is not accidental that each of the six lists of spiritual gifts basks in a context relating to love. Indeed it can be said that the teaching about spiritual gifts floats upon a sea of love. Love, in another figure, is the lubricating oil which facilitates the function of spiritual gifts.

Love is so important and so powerful that had our Lord insisted that we choose between gifts and love, the choice would obviously have been love. Thank God the way is not that narrow. Our Lord says, "Make love your aim, and desire spiritual gifts." It is like a railroad with two tracks. It is not a monorail.

CHAPTER 7

Those Lists

We catch a glimpse of God's diversity in the spiritual gifts through the Amplified New Testament. "Now there are distinctive varieties and distributions of endowments [extraordinary powers distinguishing certain Christians, due to the power of divine grace operating in their souls by the Holy Spirit] and they vary, but the (Holy) Spirit remains the same" (1 Cor. 12:4).

Those who speak of the nine gifts of the Holy Spirit have sometimes failed to see the amplitude of spiritual gifts (or gifted persons in the church) listed in Romans 12, Ephesians 4, and twice in 1 Corinthians 12. In the last list Paul mixes gifted people (apostles) along with miracles, teachers along with healings. He does make clear in 1 Corinthians 12:28 and 29 that he is referring to the ministry of individuals.

It is my firm conviction that one can take the four lists (plus three lists by inference) and compile a nearly complete scriptural list of the charismata.

Also, and this is surely in accord with Paul's emphasis upon the importance of prophecy, in the four main lists there is one common bond, one thing that ties them together as lists of the spiritual gifts. It is the consistent mention of prophecy or the persons gifted with prophecy.

In Romans 12 prophecy is mentioned. In Ephesians 4 it is prophets. In 1 Corinthians 12 it is prophecy in the first list (vv. 7-11) and prophets in the second list (v. 28).

We must also observe at this point that there are what we choose to call "lists of inference." These are found in 1 Corinthians 13:1-3, 14:6, and 14:26.

In the great love chapter, 1 Corinthians 13, Paul is comparing love with the gift of tongues in verse one. Is it too much to suppose that this comparison continues to verse three to include *giving* (also mentioned in Romans 12) and *martyrdom*?

In his corrective chapter (14) Paul describes a gathering for worship in which spiritual gifts are functioning. In verse six, true to the other lists, he mentions prophecy. But surprisingly he distinguishes between *revelation* and *knowledge*. And he adds a *doctrine*.

Then in verse 26 he includes a *psalm* (the first hint of a musical gift), a *doctrine*, a *revelation*, and an *interpretation*. It is the only time in the basic or inferred lists that prophecy is missing.

Obviously, I do not believe that the charismata can be limited to the nine gifts of the Spirit. "Gifts of healings," for example, in the original language is doubly pluralized within the so-called "nine gifts." The number may well be ninety-nine. Or more. But in this treatise I am going to deal with the four obvious and the three inferred lists.

In grouping the spiritual gifts as I do, another

question must be asked. Are gifts of leadership such as apostles and prophets to be grouped along with helps and miracles? Should there not be a distinction made between position-gifts and power-gifts? The answer I think is "yes" and "no." It is important to recognize that there are gifted men. But the Scriptures do not appear to make as fine a distinction as some today tend to do.

This is especially true in regard to prophecy —and prophets. The former is a supernatural gift; the latter, a gifted man (or woman).

Is a person with a gift of prophecy a prophet? Conversely, does a prophet have the gift of prophecy?

There are some biblical clues. For example, in 1 Samuel 10:9-13 Saul begins to prophesy. The onlookers say repeatedly, "Is Saul also among the prophets?" The implication is that he was a prophet. In 1 Corinthians 14:29-31 Paul easily shifts from "prophets" to "prophecy" and back to "prophets."

Prophets prophesy, and prophecy as a gift denotes the position of prophet. That I feel is a fair assumption.

And all this, in my view, is reason enough for moving with relative ease from the discussion of position-gifts to power-gifts.

There is also a biblical precedent. If the Holy Spirit in Scripture moves easily from one classification to the other, we should not hesitate either.

That is what He does, and this chapter is my rationale for so proceeding.

CHAPTER 8

Spiritual Gifts at Rome

Having then gifts differing according to the grace that is given to us, whether prophecy, let us prophesy according to the proportion of faith;

Or ministry, let us wait on our ministering: or he that teacheth, on teaching;

Or he that exhorteth, on exhortation: he that giveth, let him do it with simplicity; he that ruleth, with diligence; he that sheweth mercy, with cheerfulness.—Rom. 12:6-8.

Paul's epistle to the Romans includes in chapter 12 a list of the spiritual gifts. Its placement in the book is significant. It follows Romans 6, 7, 8, and Romans 12:1, 2, passages which emphasize identification with Christ and complete committal to Him. It is also locked into a context relating to the body of Christ (v. 5) and love (v. 9).

My intention is to delay treatment of prophecy until we deal with the section commonly called "the nine gifts of the Spirit." A discussion of teaching is also delayed until a later chapter.

Ministering

Now here we are confronted with "minister-ing." What is it? How does it function? The anatomy of the word makes it clear that to min-ister is to assist, to help, to communicate, to serve. Certainly there are some who minister but do not preach too well.

I recall hearing Stan Ford, a Brethren evan-gelist, speak about Jason, an obscure brother who ministered in the early church (Acts 17:5). There are certainly those today who minister also—some in the word and doctrine, some in other ways. One translation renders it, "The ability to render practical service." It may be the ability to lead others to an experience which has been preached. I count as a friend an evan-gelist who might be called an ordinary preacher, but he speaks with authority. And when he ac-tually can minister to seekers through prayer, counsel, and sometimes through the laying on of hands, he is at his strongest, his most effec-tive, and his best, ministering.

Giving

Paul also speaks of giving, in the context of spiritual gifts. Indeed, he himself may have had the gift of imparting spiritual gifts because he said to the same people earlier, "I long to see you, that I may impart unto you some spir-itual gift" (Rom. 1:11). While many will asso-ciate this gift with liberality and financial re-sources, I feel it is larger. It no doubt encom-passes more than money and goods.

But it surely does include the giving of our goods (1 Cor. 13:3) and what is commonly called Christian stewardship. Though some-times rich believers show evidence of this gift, more often it functions in the life of a very average Christian.

Once in the home of a millionaire I was asking the Lord for financial help. It did not come through the generosity of the rich man, who still remains a warm friend. Instead, during a visit in the home of an impoverished believer I had a bill pressed into my hand.

May I suggest that "God's givers" are especially in tune with God's plan for their substance?

Exhorting

Also mentioned here in Romans is exhortation. Evidently it is closely related to prophecy because it is included in the biblical meaning of the word. Generally the idea of an "encourager" comes across.

It seems clear that both Peter and Paul exercised this ability (Acts 2:40, 20:2). While oratorical qualities seem not to be especially present, exhortation can be measured by acceptance and effectiveness.

A dear man of God, who had a long and effective ministry, was in my view an extraordinarily effective exhorter. In fact, that is what he claimed to be. All through western Canada there are those who have found the Saviour through his ministry. He was jolly and sometimes jumbled in his logic, but beyond a doubt he was one of God's great exhorters.

The early Methodists appointed exhorters in their congregations. Their procedure would be worth emulating, especially when it becomes clear that the Holy Spirit is appointing exhorters.

Presiding

Finally there is he that "ruleth." From the Greek comes the idea of giving aid. The Spanish Bible uses the enlightening word "presidir," which means to preside. Most of us who are evangelicals have been to enough church services to know there are chairmen and then there are chairmen. There are song leaders and then there are song leaders. Some who have no ability to preside may be perfectly fine and sincere Christians whose only notoriety is that they make other people uncomfortable.

The apostle James exemplified the gift of ruling. In the New Testament church he was well able to calm an impetuous Peter and wisely direct the infant church.

A present-day example known to me is a youth leader who personifies the cheerful ability to preside. The congregation is at once at ease and happy when Bill rises to lead the singing or to speak. Every evangelist who seeks an effective and wide ministry must certainly have on his team a man "that ruleth." It makes for order, cheerfulness and an abundant entrance for the word of God.

And it is interesting to note that Paul, by his choice of words in the original, labels these gifts, several of them somewhat mundane and ordinary, as charismata, obviously on a par with the more spectacular and supernatural *charismata* of 1 Corinthians 12.

CHAPTER 9

On to Ephesus and Corinth

In Ephesians 4 and 1 Corinthians 11 still other gifts are mentioned.

Evangelist

First for our consideration is the gift of evangelism. It is not mentioned frequently in the Bible, but many of the dominant and more influential figures of church history were evangelists: Wesley, Whitefield, Finney, Moody, Torrey, Sunday, to name a few.

Biblically, Phillip was an evangelist, and his four daughters prophesied. Timothy evidently was not an evangelist but was told to do the work of an evangelist.

The job description of the evangelist is found in Ephesians 4:11, 12, Amplified New Testament, "And His gifts were [varied; He Himself appointed and gave men to us,] some to be apostles (special messengers), some prophets (inspired preachers and expounders), some evangelists (preachers of the Gospel, traveling missionaries), some pastors (shepherds of His flock) and teachers. His intention was the perfecting and the full equipping of the saints (His consecrated people), [that they should do] the work of ministering toward building up Christ's body (the church)."

I have known many evangelists, and no two (including myself) are the same; all have distinct varying ministries except for one common bond—they communicate the good news.

They are given "to the church." An evangelist who is so independent as to be unrelated to any visible church has forgotten the motivation of his gift. A denomination, on the other hand, which prohibits its evangelists from wider ministry has forgotten that its "administration" is but part of the transdenominational and worldwide body of Christ.

Pastor-teacher

Next come "pastor-teachers." These ministers are also given to the church, and the ministry is pastoral as well as pedagogical. (The words pastor-teacher are linked in the original language.) I should note in passing that churches, speaking biblically, may have more than one pastor at a time, and some of the most effective ministries today are "team ministries." One shall chase a thousand, two put ten thousand to flight.

Also I must interject here that a pastor may be no preacher at all. In my mind I am thinking of a wholesome, radiant, good man of God who pastors a growing, loving church. But his preaching is nondescript. He has a pastor's heart and communicates warmth. And that is what carries him. (Probably he should have his elders preach!)

The pastor (in keeping with the meaning of the word) has a shepherd's heart. He guards the church, and sometimes those of us who are in inter-church ministries think he guards it too well. But that is his function and ministry.

His teaching ministry should not be judged by its adherence to orthodox pedagogy, but rather by its effectiveness.

His control of, and guardianship over, a local congregation directly relates to his teaching and persuasive ability. Peter summarizes the duties of a pastor-teacher: "Feed the flock of God which is among you, taking the oversight thereof, not by constraint, but willingly; not for filthy lucre, but of a ready mind [being ensamples to the flock]" (1 Pet. 5:2, 3).

Apostleship

First, let us observe that the meaning of the word is "special messenger." I think that few would argue this definition since God still gives the church special messengers.

There is of course some reluctance to say that there are apostles today lest a direct lineage from Peter may be assumed. But in 1 Corinthians 15:5-7 the twelve apostles are distinguished from "all the apostles." And Revelation 21:14 makes it clear that the "twelve" are to have their names inscribed on the twelve foundations of the heavenly city. So in my opinion, there is no scriptural need for saying there should be twelve apostles today, but plenty of scriptural warrant for the continued ministry of apostles, thinking of them particularly as special messengers, or sent ones.

Though Paul possibly was not a member of the twelve (some would disagree), he claimed the signs of apostleship in signs, wonders, and mighty deeds (2 Cor. 12:12).

There were other apostles as well, e.g., Barnabas (Acts 14:14). And a comparison of 1 Thessalonians 1:1 and 2:6 also makes it clear that Paul, Timothy, and Silvanus were apostles.

Known to nearly every Christian are those of God's servants who are indeed "special messengers." Some have evangelistic gifts as well, fulfilling a specific ministry.

Probably they would reject the term apostleship in describing their ministry. The point, however, is that there are special messengers to the church. And until Christ comes there will be special messengers.

Teaching

Teaching is mentioned twice. The pastor-teacher is also mentioned in the lists. Thus we may be sure that teaching is one of the Holy Spirit's most important gifts. It is, I am sure, the Spirit-given ability to communicate effectively and impart spiritual truths. It is a solemn responsibility, and we should "be not many, teachers" (James 3:1).

Helps

And what shall I say of the gift of helps? Its meaning and usefulness are apparent. It is not a gift of leadership but of loving support. One of the blights upon Christ's church is that "we have too many chiefs and not enough Indians." I think of two men. One I will call Hank and the other Reg. Hank is a missionary. Probably he would agree that he is not at his strongest when seeking to raise up a native church among his people. But he was well nigh indispensable when we gathered for a short-term Bible school. He didn't teach but he was behind the scenes helping things go smoothly. He is that kind of a man, a helper.

Reg is another man who shuns publicity, but he makes a great head usher. He often has a breath mint for the speaker before he greets the people after a message. At our summer convention he is profoundly useful when it comes time to erect the large tent.

Probably every pastor could list the persons he has appreciated most and among them would be many with God's wondrous and most practical gift of helps. It is one we ought to "covet earnestly."

Administration

Before we move on to the gifts of inference, a word about "administration." The very presence of this gift implies that God's work is to be carefully organized, though not necessarily according to the principles and charts of the business world. Its position in the list in 1 Corinthians 12:28 would indicate that the gift of administration is of less importance than some of the gifts that have to do with the direct ministry of the Word. I am not suggesting we should honor our administrators less, but we should certainly count those who labor in the Word as worthy of double honor.

Celibacy

Further, in 1 Corinthians 7 there is scriptural warrant for suggesting that celibacy is a spiritual gift as well, and significantly Paul uses the word *charismata* in this context.

Mr. Siegfried Crossman has some interesting and worthwhile comments here. While I do not necessarily agree with all he says, I find his views helpful.

Paul specifically mentions marriage and celibacy as gifts:

> "I wish everyone could get along without marrying, just as I do. But we are not all the same. God gives some the gift of a husband or wife, and others he gives the gift of being able to stay happily unmarried" (1 Corinthians 7:7). Obviously, Paul put more value on celibacy than on marriage, for marriage seemed necessary to him only because of human passion. Today the general attitude is just the opposite—not to be married is only explainable by lack of opportunity. But whatever the changing opinion of the day, marriage and celibacy are both presented as a gift of God in 1 Corinthians.[1]

Seeking such a gift earnestly in God's will could certainly resolve the inner conflicts of unmarried or widowed Christian workers and others.

Yes, there are many charismatic abilities which are not at all spectacular. They are not necessarily supernatural so far as the uninitiated observer is concerned. But they are charismata, and they are so very much needed in the church of our Lord.

CHAPTER 10

The Gifts of Inference

As we have moved along through this discussion, I have sought to describe the nature and function of the spiritual gifts which we find mentioned in the various scriptural lists.

Now I wish to write briefly about what could be called the gifts of inference, not named but implied in Scripture.

In 1 Corinthians 13 we have Paul contrasting love with the various gifts and lauding love (though not to the exclusion of spiritual gifts).

> Though I speak with the tongues of men and of angels, and have not charity, I am become as sounding brass, or a tinkling cymbal.
>
> And though I have the gift of prophecy, and understand all mysteries, and all knowledge; and though I have all faith, so that I could remove mountains, and have not charity, I am nothing.
>
> And though I bestow all my goods to feed the poor, and though I give my body to be burned, and have not charity, it profiteth me nothing.
> —1 Cor. 13:1-3.

In verses one and two the contrast is obviously between love and tongues, prophecy, faith, etc. But in verse three Paul speaks about giving his goods to the poor. Is this a reference to the gift of giving mentioned in Romans 12? It is possible.

Then Paul suggests that if he were to give his body to be burned but did so without love, it would be unprofitable. There is the possibility here that *martyrdom* might be the ultimate function of the gift of giving. Or perhaps it is a gift in itself. Since we are in the field of inference, the implication of Paul's teaching can only be speculative. But the possibility is there.

Two other scriptures should be mentioned at this point. In 1 Corinthians 14:6 Paul describes, in a corrective context, a meeting of the local church:

> Now, brethren, if I come unto you speaking with tongues, what shall I profit you, except I shall speak to you either by revelation, or by knowledge, or by prophesying, or by doctrine?

Legitimate parts of that service included tongues, revelation, knowledge, prophesying and doctrine. Some of these manifestations I shall deal with in my chapter on the more supernatural gifts, but by inference (and it is the inference of association), Paul enumerates *revelation* and *doctrine* as distinct from the already designated gifts. In verse 26 a *psalm* is also interjected into this enlarging list of gifts in the same way, by association.

Interestingly, perhaps even surprisingly, Paul distinguishes between knowledge (I assume that he means the word of knowledge mentioned in chapter 12) and revelation.

Revelation

Revelation apparently differs from the word of knowledge.

The root word for revelation has to do with visions. I personally believe that God can and does reveal many things to the Christian so gifted. I have noticed that those who have the gift don't always understand what God is revealing to them. I think good advice to those who have this particular ability is to keep close counsel and not discuss with anyone what God is revealing. Many times the revelation is for the Christian's own direction or encouragement. There are times, however, when revelation can be shared, and the Scriptures speak of revelation in this way (1 Cor. 14:30).

Doctrine

Doctrine may well be associated with teaching, but then again it may be a gift in itself. And since we are in the realm of speculation, I'll not insist that it is indeed a gift.

I must say, however, that church history and contemporary experience do affirm that God does give to some a doctrine. It seems to me that the doctrine of justification by faith was given to Martin Luther. And is not John Wesley's name nearly synonymous with sanctification?

More recently the best-selling book by Chaplain Merlin Carothers, *Prison to Praise*, appears to indicate that God gives the rediscovery of specific doctrines to certain of His children that they might share it. Mr. Carothers, especially, seems to be publicly identified with the doctrine of praise. (Though I appreciate the book men-

tioned above, even circulate it, I hesitate to en-
dorse it fully. At one point author Carothers
suggests that in order to speak in tongues people
should let their minds go blank. That, in my
view, is a dangerous passivity, an open invitation to occult invasion and demonic deception.)

More personally, I have a close friend who
has a life ministry built around the doctrine of
death to self and the fullness of the Holy Spirit.
In all situations and before all kinds of audi-
ences, he will deliver a variation of the same
message. He is a man with a doctrine. God bless
him.

A Psalm

The psalm is the first hint we have had of
a musical gift, though prophesying, as we shall
learn later, can be done with musical instruments. I find it especially fitting that the Holy
Spirit allows a reference to music right alongside the reference to the more conventional and
recognized gifts such as tongues and interpretation.

If one takes time to study the importance
and power of praise, the possibility of a musical
spiritual gift becomes all the more obvious. David had his Asaph; Moody, his Sankey. More
particularly, the local church nearly always has
one or several musicians, though not always
Spirit-gifted.

We must not skip over the possibility raised
here (1 Cor. 14:26) that the psalms were sung
in the New Testament church as they were in
the Old Testament worship.

Now, on to more certain biblical ground.

CHAPTER 11

Supernatural Gifts

The scripture passage for our consideration is 1 Corinthians 12:7-11. The manifestations of the Holy Spirit mentioned here are generally called the "nine gifts of the Spirit." Obviously, by what has gone before you know that I believe that the gifts of the Holy Spirit are more numerous than the nine. At the same time we must clearly observe that this passage enumerates the manifestations of the Holy Spirit and they are divided under nine heads. Many students of the Word also point out that the gifts mentioned here are especially supernatural in their operation.

Raymond Kincheloe makes some helpful observations on the nature of this list:

> As far as the individual Christian is concerned, there are nine gifts of the Spirit. These are the divine enablings for Christian service. They are more than natural talents; they are supernatural powers distributed by the sovereign will of the Holy Spirit.

Gifts referring to the intellect (1 Cor. 12:8):
Wisdom
Knowledge

Gifts depending upon special faith (1 Cor. 12:9-10a):
Faith
Gifts of healings
Working of miracles
Prophecy
Discerning of spirits

Gifts referring to languages (1 Cor. 12:10b):
Tongues
Interpretation of tongues

These divisions are not arbitrary, but they are indicated by the use of the two Greek words for "another," *allos* and *heteros*. *Allos* means "another of the same kind," and this word links wisdom to knowledge, groups the next five together, and links the last two into a related pair. *Heteros* means "another of a different kind," and this word introduces faith and tongues, showing that each of these begins a new grouping respectively.[1]

Personally, I prefer to divide this list of the nine gifts along functional lines. From the functional viewpoint, there are easily discernible groups of revelation gifts, power gifts and utterance gifts.

First let us consider the gifts of revelation.

The word of wisdom

Wisdom means the correct and wise application of knowledge. The facts need not be new, but the application of them will be. The word of wisdom is just that, a word.

It is not a state of continual wisdom. The word of wisdom may possibly reside in a believer who is commonly recognized to be not especially intelligent, though this of course is certainly not a rule. Does not God delight to confound the wisdom of men?

In the early church the word of wisdom may have been possessed by Stephen and Paul. Certainly the wisdom of Stephen could not be resisted, and Paul made it clear he was not coming to the Corinthians with any human wisdom.

The most striking occasion I have ever seen where the word of wisdom was manifested was in Africa. The atmosphere was unusual and unmistakably one of revival.

The Mission chairman said something like this to the couple for whom we were praying, "You wanted to come to D—— before and the committee did not allow it even though you felt it to be God's will. Yes, God wanted you here at D——, but only for these days of convention. This is God's will for you."

The missionary couple who had wanted to be appointed to that city as resident missionaries were overwhelmed. Indeed, the wife cried out in surprise as the word of wisdom was given. Suddenly the plan for their lives fitted together beautifully.

The word of knowledge

We should first of all remind ourselves that this gift is a supernatural one. The knowledge referred to here is not gained by study nor is it the product of human effort. (Though of course we must not forget to study as the Scriptures command us.)

Note also that it is *a word* of knowledge, not a continual state of knowledge. As with the word of wisdom, this gift also may appear among those of limited mental ability as well as among church leaders and officers.

Moreover, knowledge of the word should not be confused with the word of knowledge. One is the result of long study and devotion to the Bible. The other is a supernatural operation of the Holy Spirit.

In the Old Testament Samuel told Saul where his asses would be found (1 Sam. 9:19, 20). Elisha revealed the location of the Syrian army in the same way, using knowledge given him from God (2 Kings 6:9). And in the New Testament we find Ananias and Sapphira unable to deceive Peter and the early church. By the Spirit of God Peter knew of their deceitful behavior. And God's judgment fell upon them. The word of knowledge may also have been functioning in Paul at Lystra. He saw faith in a crippled man; he knew deep within that the man had faith to be healed. Thus he commanded him to stand upon his feet. And the man leaped and walked.

A friend who is a pastor related this story: On one occasion in an atmosphere of revival God showed him that a certain rebellious young man for whom they were concerned would come screeching up to the house in his car, that he would come through the door without speaking, and that he would take the chair in the corner. But he would then break down and get right with God. As I recall, the pastor also announced to others what was going to happen.

Shortly afterward a car did come to a screeching stop outside the house, the sullen young man did come in, and he did choose the chair in the corner. And then he began to weep brokenly before the Lord.

Such a spiritual manifestation is, to me, a word of knowledge.

Discerning of spirits

This gift is commonly called discerning. But as far as the biblical lists are concerned, there is no such gift as discernment. It is discerning of spirits.

There are four classes of spirits mentioned in the Word of God: the human spirit, the Holy Spirit, angelic spirits, and demonic spirits. The person gifted with the discerning of spirits will often know which spirit is at work. It is probably the most needed gift of all in this day of occult invasion.

The gift is also vitally related to the casting out of demons. Obviously the discerning of spirits was functioning in Philip when in Samaria he was casting out demons who protested with loud voices. Paul seemed also to have had the discerning of spirits in his life. The fortune-telling girl had followed them for days. But one day Paul turned. The enemy was caught like a rat out of his hole. And the demon was driven out.

In my personal introduction to the spiritual gifts, this gift was the first I was privileged to see in operation. I had heard of the ministry of a certain brother and I wanted to invite him to my church, even though I was afraid as well because of the supernatural things which I had heard accompanied his ministry.

After preaching once in our church he said to me, "You have problems in your church, don't you?" Then he named the two individuals involved. They were the most difficult people in the church to handle.

Then I was more afraid—if this man knew that about these people, what did he know about me? My fear, by the way, was a reflection of my own need.

Through the years since then this brother has consistently demonstrated the gift of discerning of spirits and has ordered his life and ministry in a Christ-adorning way.

Though discerning of spirits directly relates to the ministry of exorcism, it is very helpful in understanding the many intricacies of satanic working. It also has a connection to divine healing since some diseases are demonic in nature (Luke 8:36).

I should also make clear that any believer who believes can cast out demons according to Mark 16:17. Exorcism is possible for all believers. Discerning of spirits is available to some, as God wills.

While space forbids any lengthy discussion of deliverance at this point, the commonly accepted way of identifying satanic working is by the words of oppression, obsession, and possession. According to my understanding, oppression is exterior from the person involved, though it may be physical as well as spiritual (Acts 10:38). Obsession is in the mind, and it begins when the oppressed person believes the devil's lie. Possession is satanic control of the body. Christ's power to dislodge the enemy is complete.

For the Greek students reading this I should add that I realize that scripturally, people are simply described as "demonized." Nevertheless, in experience, oppression, obsession and possession are counseling terms that can be used to describe the various needs of people and the various stages of satanic control and invasion.

Next we shall consider the gifts of power— namely, faith, gifts of healings, and miracles.

Faith

"To another faith." In Romans Paul declares that God has given to all men "a measure of faith" (Rom. 12:6). This is obviously true and men tend to put their innate faith in many things, such as money, education, politics and religion. But it can also be put in a chair. It is the ability that all men have and it saves no one.

There is also saving faith which brings a man to vibrant life in Christ. But what we have under consideration here is a special gift of faith that enables Christian believers to do exploits.

George Mueller was one of history's great believers. For many years he fed thousands of orphans without soliciting money or food from anyone. By his exercise of faith alone they lived in the miraculous nearly every day.

Hudson Taylor, too, who sent hundreds of missionaries to China, simply believed that God's work done in God's way would never lack God's supply. I find it easy to believe that God gave to these servants a gift of faith.

In Acts 3 Peter is confronted with a mountain of impossibility. He did not lay hands on the lame man. Nor did he whip out his vial of anointing oil. Instead Peter spoke to the mountain of lameness. He commanded it to move! "In the name of Jesus Christ of Nazareth, rise up and walk." Daring words! With explosive results.

Similarly Peter spoke the word of faith to Aeneas, "Jesus Christ maketh thee whole: rise and make thy bed." When Dorcas died, there was no anointing oil or laying on of hands. (Though both procedures are biblical and proper as the Holy Spirit leads.) But there was the spoken command: "Tabitha, arise." She opened her eyes, and when she saw Peter she sat up.

I believe that Latin Americans could teach us a great deal about faith. In 1969-70 the Jimenez brothers, Eugenio and Raimundo, conducted, along with other evangelists, Campañas de Fe (Campaigns of Faith) throughout the major cities of Colombia. God used these brothers in a remarkable way; their procedures were very simple. They secured public places and then preached a dual message—the forgiveness of sins and the healing of the body. Traditionally Roman Catholic Colombians had no trouble receiving and experiencing the miraculous. On very few occasions did the evangelists touch the people or lay hands on them. But there were many miracles. And the impact on the nation—incalculable.

For example, in the city of Medellin, a beautiful city of one million people, as many as 10,000 gathered outside the bull ring to hear Raimundo Jimenez. Afterward in nearly every barrio of the great city evangelicals were on the move. A campaign of faith had pried the city open. And for years it had been a very difficult city for evangelical work.

I should perhaps explain that evangelistic campaigns including an emphasis on divine healing have much more respectability and prestige in Latin America than North America where more conservative forms of evangelicalism are predominant.

Should we not remind ourselves that the gift of faith is one of God's most powerful gifts? We should covet it earnestly in His will.

Gifts of healings

The second gift of power is doubly pluralized,

gifts of healings. Matthew lists many kinds of sicknesses (4:23, 24), and we may assume that not every gift of healing will be the same. That would be contrary to God's dealing in many other areas. There may be as many gifts of healing as there are kinds of sicknesses.

Perhaps this is the place to say also that the gifts of the Holy Spirit are intended to adorn the doctrine of Christ. Many abuses have taken place, especially in the ministry of healing, and no doubt this will continue, but we should not let abuses rob us of the multiplied gifts of healings that God intends for His church.

Sometimes in the Scripture there is a merging of the gifts. For example, when Peter spoke the healing words to the man at the gate of the beautiful temple, there was a manifestation of faith, healing, and the miraculous. It follows in that event that as many as three gifts may have been functioning at the same time.

We should also distinguish between the healing ministry of any believer and a gift of healing as a special ministry. "These signs shall follow them that believe ... in my name they shall lay hands upon the sick and they shall recover." Any believer may pray effectively for the sick, but God gives to some of His children, as He wills, special powers of healing.

The gift of miracles

Miracles are recorded in the lives of many biblical characters, and the majority of the miracles have no connection with healing. However, no treatment of the gift of miracles can avoid reference to healing. I am inclined to view a miracle, when it refers to healing, as an instantaneous act of God. Whereas healings in general, which are not necessarily a manifestation of the gift of miracles, may take a period of time to be consummated even though they are miraculous.

The Holy Spirit also uses a miracle to initiate a testimony or to give visible credentials to God's servants.

The following is not intended as a claim to the gift of miracles. But it is an illustration of the usefulness of a miracle. I was once called to minister in a church which was about to slide into what might be called "charismatic error." In view of this tendency everyone there was very anxious to come to the altar to pray. Accordingly I delivered night by night the basic material of this book, but without giving a single invitation because I felt teaching was needed.

And one night there was a confirming miracle. The Lord had given us the promise, "Tomorrow I will do wonders among you." The service of that "tomorrow" passed without any specific answer to prayer.

But after the service, through the front door of that isolated frontier church came a new convert called Ray. He was five months old in the Lord, and suffering very much. The doctors had placed steel pins in one knee so that he was able to use it again but could not bend it. But now he had fallen, his other knee had suffered serious injury, and the medical authorities wanted to pin that leg as well.

Not wanting to be entirely immobile, Ray told them no. He decided he would pray. He had already asked for prayer and we had said, "Certainly, as the Lord leads."

We sensed the moment had arrived. As Ray came through the door his pain was obvious. And an elder and I both moved toward the pastor. "Let's pray for Ray now."

The three of us placed our hands upon his knee and prayed simply. Our eyes were closed but his were wide open. Were we massaging his knee or something? he wondered.

No. He just felt the Lord taking corrective measures in his knee. He felt things going back into place. It was a remarkable healing.

Not surprisingly, the church listened to all I had to say, was corrected, and went on to experience spiritual gifts and to maintain spiritual equilibrium as well. A miracle had confirmed a ministry.

I have a friend, formerly a missionary to Peru, who has had many miraculous experiences.

In impossible circumstances and against all odds, he was granted an audience with Pope Paul. The conversation was beneficial but afterward he had one regret—he had not given a vibrant witness for Christ. So he prayed for another chance. And while bishops and other VIP's were unable to see the pontiff, the evangelical pastor was ushered in again for a private audience. The second time he was able to speak effectively about his relationship to Christ. Certainly miraculous events in the life of an evangelical pastor!

During his missionary career this same friend boarded a plane on his way to a special campaign. There was only one seat left, so he sat down beside Peru's Roman Catholic man of the year—who was on his way to speak in the same city. However, the man of the year was uncertain about his speech. Solicitously, perhaps mischievously, the missionary offered him a message. The Peruvian was agreeable so the missionary gave him the outline for an

72

evangelistic message on Mary the Mother
of Jesus.

Later the Protestant missionary listened to
his own evangelistic message being delivered
to a mass rally by the Roman Catholic man
of the year. A miracle? I think so.

In Corrie ten Boom's best-selling book, *The
Hiding Place*, she describes a bottle of medicine
that was the prisoners' only source of relief in
a Nazi prison camp. It did not run dry, no matter
how often it was used, until help from another
source arrived. Then and only then did the bottle
go dry. And the incident is but one of the many
miracles in Miss ten Boom's life.

I could cite many other incidents, but let it
suffice to say that the day of miracles is not
past. Moreover, miracles are a manifestation
of the Holy Spirit that can properly be coveted
earnestly in God's will.

The gifts of the Holy Spirit are the power-
oriented equipment of the church. They are not
by any means the evidence of spirituality and
disciplined Christianity.

Prophecy

Though the word of wisdom and the word
of knowledge might both be considered in part
utterance gifts, there can be no doubt that prophecy is an utterance gift. This gift, that Paul
declares should be sought above all others, can
be defined in two ways.

First of all, there is the meaning of the words
"to tell," "to tell forth," and even "to forthtell."
There is also the scriptural definition "... he
that prophesieth speaketh unto men to edifica-
tion, exhortation, and comfort" (1 Cor. 14:3).

Then in the Old Testament there is the reference to prophesying with musical instruments (1 Chron. 25:3). In that case prophesying did not need to be verbal.

But in these pages we will focus on the New Testament teaching about prophecy. To begin with, prophecy should in no case be considered as a material addition to the Bible. "For I testify unto every man that heareth the words of prophecy of this book, If any man shall add unto these things, God shall add unto him the plagues that are written in this book" (Rev. 22:18). This warning no doubt refers specifically to the book of Revelation; but Revelation, we must remember, is part of the whole Bible.

It also needs to be made clear that prophecy is not teaching, though it can be a source of learning. "For ye may all prophesy one by one, that all may learn, and all may be comforted" (1 Cor. 14:31).

In passing we must also note that 1 Corinthians 12:28 distinguishes between prophecy and teaching. "And God hath set some in the church, first apostles, secondarily prophets, thirdly teachers, after that miracles. . . . "

Preaching is intended to be prophetic as indicated by the very meaning of the word—to tell forth. It would be too much to suggest that all preaching has the prophetic quality, but some definitely does. And all of us have heard it. Unctionized preaching is a form of prophecy, perhaps the dominant form.

Prophecy also may be an utterance type of spiritual manifestation. In fact, Paul often associated it with tongues because of its similarity. Prophecy, however, will be an utterance in the vernacular of the people to whom it is directed. "Do not neglect the gift which is in you, [that special inward endowment] which was directly imparted to you [by the Holy Spirit] by prophetic utterance when the elders laid their hands upon you [at your ordination]" (1 Tim. 4:14, Amplified New Testament). That was Paul's word on prophecy to Timothy.

There is also the possibility that prophecy will spill over into the future. Those who resist this possibility must explain why it was that Agabus, in a New Testament context, prophesied repeatedly about Paul's future.

In October of 1972 God was pleased to send revival to the evangelical church in Bobo-Dioulasso, Upper Volta. Some time later we learned through an oblique reference made during a time of sharing that a prophecy had been given and it had announced the visitation of God beforehand.

While I think it is only realistic to admit the futuristic and utterance possibilities of prophecy, it is wise to place most emphasis on the preaching ministry. That is by far the most important and was, without doubt, the reason Paul stressed prophecy so strongly.

Other facts relating to prophecy are made clear in 1 Corinthians 14. Prophecy is equated with tongues and interpretation (14:5). It also edifies the church (v. 4), is for them that believe (v. 22), and reveals the secrets of the heart (v. 25).

The apostle further specifies that in a church service all may prophesy if they wish. This is in contrast to tongues where only three are allowed to participate and then only when interpretation is available (v. 31).

Also, prophecy is subject to the prophets; in no case is the prophet forced to speak the message publicly.

In a recent series of meetings in a church in Idaho there was a large response to my message on how to be filled with the Holy Spirit. While we were praying for the people with the laying on of hands, the pastor received a prophecy. Since it was a word of warning to certain parents there present, he took the couple aside and shared the matter with them. I was struck with the choice the pastor made, subjecting the prophecy to his own will and delivering it discretely at a more appropriate time.

In 1 Thessalonians 5:20 St. Paul further elaborates on prophecy, indicating that it must not be despised and perhaps implying that in charismatic congregations frequent manifestations may cause some to despise the gift. In verse 21 Paul's exhortation is to prove all things. False prophets there obviously are. And if there are false prophets, then of course there is false prophecy. It is hardly accidental that the word of caution comes exactly here.

It is commonly understood that prophets whose predictions do not come true are false prophets, while those whose predictions do come true are genuine. But another criterion must be added. Prophets whose words come true but draw the people's hearts away from God are also false (Deut. 13:1-3).

The tests then for prophecy are several. First, does the verbal content agree in all points with the Scripture? Second, even if the content is biblical, what is the spirit like? Is it jarring? Abrasive? If so, then something is still wrong regardless of the content.

Larry Christenson makes an interesting note at this point:

> A neighboring pastor told us about an experience which he once had with the discern-

ment of spirits. Two strange women came to his church one day, and in the course of the meeting stood up and prophesied. The words were scriptural, and yet he felt like a whole battery of fire alarms started to go off inside him. He leaned over to an older pastor who was sitting next to him, and said, "What is it about those women?" The older pastor answered, "The words are true, but the spirit is false." [2]

Trying the spirit would be the final test. "Believe not every spirit, but try the spirits whether they are of God: because many false prophets are gone out into the world. Hereby know ye the Spirit of God: Every spirit that confesseth that Jesus Christ is come in the flesh is of God: and every spirit that confesseth not that Jesus Christ is come in the flesh is not of God: and this is that spirit of antichrist, whereof ye have heard that it should come; and even now already is it in the world" (1 John 4:1-3).

We will go into this more in the chapter on testing tongues, but I must insert here that trying the spirits involves *four possible responses*: Only a constant affirmative *yes* denotes the spirit to be of God; but a reluctant affirmation, evasive silence, or an open denial that the Lord Jesus Christ came in the flesh all mean that the spirit is not of God.

Moreover, scripture does not say, "Try the prophets." It says, "Try the spirits."

Tongues

Since I shall treat the gift of tongues separately in various ways, we will not go into a biblical description of it here. It is because Paul dealt with it correctively in the Corinthian church that there is more biblical material.

Suffice it to say that I do certainly believe and have seen that there is a beautiful, wholesome, scriptural, Christ-adorning gift of tongues. I well remember hearing for the first time singing in tongues from the lips of a teenager. It was a lilting, flowing melody that brought a rush of tears to my eyes.

Interpretation of tongues

The gift of interpreting tongues is a potentially vital part of the spiritual life of one who speaks in tongues; otherwise he who speaks in tongues can have no public ministry with tongues. The command is specific. He that speaks in tongues is to pray that he will interpret (1 Cor. 14:13), and the implication is that it probably is God's will that he should also interpret.

It is commonly agreed by those who write on these matters that interpretation of tongues should not be considered translation. Those who are unable to speak in tongues sometimes have the ability to interpret, or vice versa.

The interpretation will follow the tongues utterance and will be in the vernacular of the people involved.

Not all interpret, Paul makes clear, but those who speak in tongues should pray that they will interpret.

CHAPTER 12

Biblical Tongues

Only once in my life have I been told what I could or could not preach. And as you can imagine, things were very tense in that Ontario church when the pastor forbade me to preach about the Holy Spirit, though I let him know I really wanted to do so.

More recently the brother who opposed me then has not only come into a new experience with the Holy Spirit, but he also speaks in tongues as well.

Just prior to writing this book I asked him why it is that people get so excited about speaking in tongues. His eyes brimmed with tears and he answered simply, "Because it is so very wonderful!"

I cannot help but accept the testimony from one who once collided with me theologically and spiritually. The change has been remarkable.

But why is a biblical experience of tongues so wonderful? Obviously tongues is the only gift which is nearly completely subjective in nature. A gift of healing or helps, for example, is objective; it ministers to others. Tongues alone among the gifts has a major benefit for the possessor's private life and experience with Christ.

Also a definition is in order: Speaking in tongues is an ability given by the Holy Spirit which enables a Christian to speak in a language unknown to him, which at the same time immensely benefits him and may benefit others.

Biblically, tongues is anticipated in 1 Corinthians 12 before it is mentioned. It is included in what Paul has in mind in verse three: "Wherefore I give you to understand, that no man speaking by the Spirit of God calleth Jesus accursed: and that no man can say that Jesus is the Lord, but by the Holy Ghost."

Paul mentions here the phenomenon which we may call spirit-speaking. He suggests that a man may speak by various spirits (e.g., human, demonic, divine). Then he says that no one speaking that way by the Spirit of God will ever call Jesus Lord but by the Holy Spirit.

I think that this text has been consistently overlooked. It is a key verse on the subject of spiritual gifts, especially in view of the context that follows it. And because of its emphasis on *speaking*, it is a key verse on speaking in tongues.

A very great deal of sorrow, confusion and delusion could be avoided if Christians generally insisted that tongues-speaking spirits manifesting themselves in people be tested. (I will describe in detail in chapter 15 exactly how I believe this test should be applied.)

The rankest unbeliever could call Jesus Lord with his lips. But *speaking by any spirit* but the Holy Spirit he absolutely could not continue to do so.

I am thus suggesting that scripturally God never intended us to accept spiritual utterance without question, without spiritual testing.

Apart from spirit-testing as outlined in 1 John 4:1-3, there is the possibility that a spirit utterance may be tested through the function of spiritual gifts, especially the word of knowledge, revelation, and the discerning of spirits.

Recently in my office I was called upon to test a tongue. Prior to the application of the test commanded in 1 John 4:1-3, the young man and I prayed. And I sensed within me that the tongue we were about to test was genuine. The verbal test confirmed to my heart what I already knew.

The incident was extemely interesting because about 18 months previously two tongues-speaking demons had been exorcised from the same young man.

Next, in verse ten, it is clear that tongues is one of the Holy Spirit's gifts. And certainly the Holy Spirit gives only the very best. Tongues cannot be measured by any other standard. When it is genuine it is a beautiful gift from the Holy Spirit.

The next mention of tongues occurs in verse 28. The order in verse 28 suggests that apostleship is first and diversities of tongues is last. If there is an ascending stairway, tongues is the bottom step. To quarrel with that is to attach undue importance to the gift.

"Diversities" suggests a variety of tongues, perhaps as in 1 Corinthians 13:1, the tongues of men and angels. But even those tongues without love are valueless.

I have earlier pointed out (chapter 6) that not all will speak in tongues. And to avoid that truth is to move off the safety of biblical ground. Some speak in tongues and some do not.

I recall a lady tugging at my arm after a message on the gifts of the Spirit. "My husband," she said, "wants to know if tongues is necessary. Yes or no?" I didn't answer her to her satisfaction because she wanted an unbiblical answer. "Yes" and "no" are both wrong when God says "maybe," when He divides severally as He wills.

In 13:8 there can be no mistaking it—tongues shall cease. The most ardent opponents believe they have ceased already. I think it is safer to be in the middle and say that they haven't passed away yet but they will.

In chapter 14:1, without excluding tongues, Paul says "desire spiritual gifts." A sincere Christian could desire tongues, then, as one of the gifts but should especially desire prophecy.

Paul next proceeds to explain the function of speaking in tongues. The tongues-speaker speaks to God; in the spirit he speaks mysteries, he edifies himself.

Paul says, "I would that ye all spake with tongues." But making that a doctrine is not only dishonest but dangerous. He immediately adds, "but rather that ye prophesied: for greater is he that prophesieth than he that speaketh with tongues, except he interpret, that the church may receive edifying."

Tongues without interpretation do not profit the church, but tongues-speakers are to pray that they will interpret (v. 13).

Praying in tongues is a prayer of the human spirit which leaves the understanding unfruitful (v. 14). It is not to be done to the exclusion of prayer with the intellect (v. 15).

Singing can be done in tongues or with the understanding. And Paul adds that praying and singing are not the only things that can be done with the spirit (v. 15). Blessings can also be given (v. 16). A friend of mine, and a frequent visitor to our summer conventions, told this story. He was ministering to a group and the flow of the conversation was anti-tongues. Somewhat grieved he explained a little bit to them and then he said to them, "Listen, I am going to bless you in tongues." He proceeded to do it. And the whole group was moved to tears by the sweetness of God's presence.

First Corinthians 14:18 is another passage often lifted out of its context. "I thank my God, I speak with tongues more than ye all." Paul was a great tongues-speaker. But he continues, "Yet in the church I had rather speak five words with my understanding, that my voice might teach others also, than ten thousand words in an unknown tongue."

In verse 20 he suggests that those who promote tongues are being childish and he appeals for maturity.

Verse 22 is many times ignored by writers or speakers who insist that tongues are the only evidence of being filled with the Holy Spirit. Tongues, Paul says, are not for a sign to those that believe. They are a sign for the unbeliever. "Wherefore tongues are for a sign, not to them that believe, but to them that believe not." Departure from this biblical ground has been disastrous as we shall see in a later chapter.

And in case you missed it, *tongues are for a sign to unbelievers*. If we are to oppose tongues completely, what about the unbelievers? What about them?

In verse 23 the apostle tells the tongues-speakers that everyone will think they are mad if they all come together and speak at the same time.

He doesn't rule it out completely (v. 26). Two or three may speak in tongues, and then only with interpretation. And if there is no interpreter, then let him keep silence in the church (vv. 27-28).

I must pause to observe that tongues is the only gift that the Holy Spirit puts restrictive controls on: two or at the most three and then only with an interpreter. Prophecy appears to be slightly controlled. Contemporary church history confirms the wisdom of the Holy Spirit since undisciplined speaking in tongues probably causes more church problems than all other manifestations of spiritual gifts put together.

First Corinthians 14:32 speaks directly of prophecy but includes teaching about tongues. Just because a person feels a surge within to speak, there is no reason to believe the Holy Spirit is grieved if the tongues message is not given. The spirit of the prophet is subject to the prophet. The fruit of the Spirit is self-control. In self-control the charismatic Christian calls the plays. He is the quarterback.

Verse 33 certainly provokes thought. God is not the author of confusion. Agreed. But if He isn't, who is?

Now in verse 34 we come to a passage which does not clearly refer to tongues but may well refer to them. "Let your women keep silence in the churches: for it is not permitted unto them to speak; but they are commanded to be under obedience, as also saith the law." If women are not allowed to speak in tongues in the church, the possibilities of abuse are considerably reduced.

Paul says women are to be under obedience (1 Cor. 14:34). Earlier he had said, "For this cause ought the woman to have power on her head because of the angels" (1 Cor. 11:10).

A woman without the protective umbrella of a man's authority is vulnerable. She is open to the satanic attack of fallen angels and may easily give ground to the enemy. She is also more easily deceived.

Those involved in deliverance ministry will attest that victims of demonic invasion are much more frequently women than men. Vulnerability is the reason. All the more reason for our dear wives and sisters to be under the authority of understanding, compassionate Christian men.

While this passage about women keeping silence in the church may not be specifically referring to speaking in tongues in church, because of the general tenor of Paul's remarks, I think it would be good advice for any local congregation to follow.

Paul sums it up with these beautifully balanced phrases:

> Wherefore, brethren, covet to prophesy, and forbid not to speak with tongues. Let all things be done decently and in order.—1 Cor. 14:39, 40.

"Cool it, calm down, take it easy. Don't seek tongues unless the Lord reveals that the gift is for you. But it should not be forbidden either." This is the feeling I get from Paul.

When Paul says, "Covet earnestly the best gifts," he appends that advice to a list that terminates with tongues and interpretation of tongues. The implication is clear. Seek the best gifts; seek to be special messengers, to preach, to teach, to work miracles. Paul, in my view, is emphasizing the top of the list, the best gifts.

But it does not follow that tongues is the worst gift. How could any beautiful gift of the Holy Spirit be so labelled? But the comparative importance of tongues is clearly minimized.

"Seek not, forbid not," as some are saying, is good biblical advice. And in essence, this is the "third view" of tongues.

And if this advice be followed, will not tongues disappear? Certainly not. If the pattern of Acts holds true, some, but not all, who are filled with the Holy Spirit will speak in tongues. And so long as Christians do not seek tongues *per se*, but only the encounter with the living Christ which is the fullness of the Spirit, then a biblical order has developed and is being followed.

I should also pause to make clear that there is a time and a place for seeking the gift of speaking in tongues.

If a sincere Christian believer recognizes that "not all speak with tongues," then prayerfully submits himself to the will of God, and still feels that the Lord wills that gift for his life, he then may certainly pray with assurance and have every expectation of receiving a true charisma of the Holy Spirit. "God also bearing them witness, both with signs and wonders, and with divers miracles, and gifts of the Holy Ghost, according to his own will" (Heb. 2:4). "But all these worketh that one and the selfsame Spirit, dividing to every man severally as he will" (1 Cor. 12:11).

If He "spared not his own Son, but delivered him up for us all, how shall he not with him freely give us all things?" (Rom. 8:32).

Now let us suppose: If a believer who has

never been exposed to the modern tongues controversy were exposed to 1 Corinthians 12, 13, and 14 for the first time and then asked to summarize Paul's feeling about tongues, what would he say? I believe he would say something like this, "Paul was trying to restrain tongues, to put the brakes on them, without stamping them out or denying their validity."

And this I believe. Paul was definitely not tramping on the gas. He was hitting the brakes, carefully but firmly.

I have wondered, too, if Paul were with us today, what would be his emphasis? Where would he fellowship? I doubt that he would be jetting from city to city—as one of my friends says, "laying the tongues trip on people." But he wouldn't be happy either among those who insist that the sign gifts are not for today. His ministry of healing and his speaking in tongues would be an embarrassment there.

I rather think Paul would be out in the middle somewhere.

And we should be too!

CHAPTER 13

False Gifts

Thank God for this scripture: "If a son shall ask bread of any of you that is a father, will he give him a stone? or if he ask a fish, will he for a fish give him a serpent? or if he shall ask an egg, will he offer him a scorpion? If ye then, being evil, know how to give good gifts unto your children: how much more shall your heavenly Father give the Holy Spirit to them that ask him?" (Luke 11:11-13).

But can it be claimed as certain assurance that those who insist upon a tongues experience contrary to scriptures will never get a stone or serpent?

If this scripture can be used in this way, why then the manifestation of false gifts on every side? For example, I know personally a former preacher who finally discovered his gifts were not of God. I was in the counselling room when he was converted. During his Bible college days I had occasional contact with him. He began working in what would be called a non-charismatic evangelical denomination. He left

88

to pastor a Pentecostal church because of his speaking in tongues and also other "gifts" such as the ability to identify the sins of the people in the congregation. At the same time his marriage deteriorated. He finally left the ministry. In his case there were also frequent outbursts of obscenity and later abject backsliding.

Finally in desperation he came to his former friends, so-called non-charismatic pastors. In a deliverance which lasted several hours these pastors drove out eight demons, many of them naming themselves as false gifts, several of them speaking in tongues.

Experiences like that hardly engender an attitude of trust toward the charismatics by the so-called non-charismatics.

Liberating charismatics from their false tongues by exorcism is not something that happens in isolated cases. Such incidents are increasingly frequent and more books are certain to be written along this line. It's now possible to meet Christians who have been "delivered from tongues."

While false gifts seem especially to involve tongues and to some degree prophecy, other gifts are involved. In fact, Satan seems to have a strategy set which involves the counterfeit of every true gift of the Holy Spirit.

Why so many false tongues? First, it is the focal point, the pressure point. *To teach or imply that all believers must or could speak in tongues carries the Christian off biblical ground and opens the door to stones and serpents.*

Luke 11:11-13 is carefully claimed by the charismatic movement. There'll be no stones or serpents, the seekers are assured.

Yet I would estimate twenty-five percent of

the deliverance ministry God has allowed me over the years has involved the extrication of deceived people from the false charismatic manifestations. Most of the cases included demonic tongues.

One brother who has tested tongues for forty years says that in his experience nine out of ten were false.

In a recently published article one of our contemporaries cites a similar statistic: Ninety percent of the tongues he and his colleagues have tested have been false.[1] In my own experience perhaps eighty percent of the tongues manifestations that I have had to deal with have been false.

Still I doubt that the statistics tell the whole story. Because people with genuine gifts and healthy spiritual life do not come for counselling nearly so frequently. But there is no denying that the devil has been having a field day among charismatics. His penetration, whatever the percentage, appears to be massive.

But to face the issue of false gifts, stones and serpents, the open door to satanic penetration is in the merging of the work of the Holy Spirit *which is for all* with a spiritual gift that is given *only to some* as God wills. The resulting confusion is very often tragic.

Let hungry hearted believers ask only for the Holy Spirit in His fullness, allowing the sovereign Spirit to distribute and choose the gifts as He wills and the door to stones and serpents is slammed shut.

Another case history is important at this point. A teenager was subjected to the overtures of a radical charismatic group, a group which in turn would certainly be rejected by mainline groups of Pentecostals.

He allowed hands to be laid on him and "saw" a bright light. Later in a "Canadian revival" atmosphere, as distinct from "charismatic" atmosphere, the youth felt a bondage he could not escape until he made a verbal commitment much like this, "In the name of the Lord Jesus Christ I now refuse, repudiate and renounce completely any and all spirits of false prophecy from —— (naming the false prophet). And I send them to the abyss in Jesus' name." He was instantly liberated and sensed within that the "charismatic" bondage had been broken.

In addition to the departure from biblical ground, there are other reasons why individuals receive false gifts.

The second is that there sometimes is occult bondage in the lives of God's children, sometimes clinging to them from several generations back. For more information on this problem see Kurt Koch's book *Occult Bondage and Deliverance* (Grand Rapids, Michigan: Kregel Publishers).

If the person is not clear from the encumbrances of an occult past or present, the possibilities of receiving false gifts is very high. Spirit forces with occult capabilities can easily switch to imitate gifts of the Holy Spirit.

Another reason for the epidemic of spurious charismata today is the tendency of untaught spiritual novices to seek "the baptism of the Holy Spirit" while still entangled in sin.

A teenage girl was actively seeking the "baptism" and living in fornication at the same time. She received all right. But it was a tongues-speaking serpent that had to be exorcised.

In summary, departure from biblical ground must be called the most dangerous aberration.

After ministering in Latin America repeatedly and visiting other parts of the world, I have no doubt that Roman Catholics are changing, that there is more openness than ever before to the gospel. And we rejoice over this.

However, in Kevin Ranaghan's book *Catholic Pentecostals*, he documents some of the unusual events which are taking place among charismatic Roman Catholics.

One of the witnesses in the book vouches for "a greater realization of the eucharist as sacrifice . . . a deep devotion to Mary." [2] All this through tongues.

Now if the Bible is to be believed, the fact is that Christ was once offered and He is the *only* mediator between God and man.

Some other spirit may indeed promote a glow of good will over the eucharistic reenactment of the death of Christ and devotion to Mary, the great mediatrix. However, it can hardly be the Holy Spirit of Almighty God who inspired the New Testament.

Another case in point, carefully observed by a pastor-friend, proceeded in this manner. In a Catholic center in a Canadian city a Roman Catholic nun was seeking "the baptism" of the Holy Spirit. She was suddenly and powerfully overcome and began to speak in tongues and to manifest great excitement, joy and exuberance. The priest in charge was then careful to point out, "See how powerful Mary is. We prayed to Mary for this."

These comments should not be construed by any means as a blanket denunciation of the charismatic movement among Roman Catholics. Their brand of "pentecostalism" may be the dominant kind in twenty-five years. But these examples make it clear that false gifts no doubt exist among them as well.

There is yet another reason why error and false gifts penetrate the assembly of God's children. In Paul's first epistle to Timothy, three times the aged apostle lays it on the line concerning error:

> Neither give heed to fables and endless genealogies, which minister questions, rather than godly edifying which is in faith: so do. Now the end of the commandment is charity out of a pure heart, and of a good conscience, and of faith unfeigned: from which some having swerved have turned aside unto vain jangling. —1 Tim. 1:4-6.
>
> Holding faith, and a good conscience; which some having put away concerning faith have made shipwreck.—1 Tim. 1:19.
>
> Now the Spirit speaketh expressly, that in the latter times some shall depart from the faith, giving heed to seducing spirits, and doctrines of devils; speaking lies in hypocrisy; having their conscience seared with a hot iron. —1 Tim. 4:1-2.

The dominant emphasis is conscience, a good conscience. Like a faulty compass, an off-center conscience opens the door to error. An ignored conscience does the same. And false gifts come marching in.

That spirituality has no continuing demonstrable relationship to spiritual gifts I have illustrated in these pages. How much more reason, then, should the man of God have a clean heart and a good conscience before coveting earnestly any spiritual gift.

Personally, I have learned this lesson a very hard way. Along with friends I entered into a project about which I had qualms of conscience.

The results, had I studied Paul's words to Timothy, were predictable. One of the participating brethren was carried into error, charismatic error in fact, and I have no other recourse but to hold myself partly to blame.

The Holy Spirit is holy. He does not rush to fill or equip anyone. The enemy, on the other hand, is an unclean spirit. He does not mind an unclean vessel—in fact, the more filthy, the better.

Death to self, identification with Jesus Christ in His death, burial and resurrection, a clean heart and a good conscience are indispensable safeguards for the Christian who would be charismatic. There are no shortcuts, no easy ways.

One charismatic spokesman (we will omit the footnote in this case) has some alarming things to say. While it would be a mistake to attribute his views to all charismatics, the essence of it is that gifts are gifts, period, and that there are no requirements of holiness at all in receiving the spiritual gifts.

Spiritual gifts may indeed come without cleansing, sanctification, without a clean heart and a good conscience. But from whence will they come? And from whom?

Still another reason for the epidemic of false gifts today is that spiritual things, both good and bad, are contagious. And the evil will always run faster than the good.

The contagiousness of spiritual things is often unrecognized. But it is a vital factor in biblical Christianity. Timothy accompanied Paul for definite reasons—to be taught and to receive the spiritual imprint of Paul's ministry. Indeed Peter specifically says, "As every man hath received the gift, even so minister the same one to another, as good stewards of the manifold grace of God" (1 Pet. 4:10).

Some false gifts are only fleshly. That is not to say they are not dangerous or grievous to our Lord.

A young fellow once confided to me, "The young people at our church think I speak in tongues, but I don't really. It's just me." How many "charismatic" manifestations are purely fleshly, I cannot say, but some are. It would be very foolish to immediately assume that all false gifts are satanic counterfeits. The carnal nature is capable of a very great deal and finds the imitation of speaking in tongues no great difficulty.

It is generally stated that the charismatic movement is opposed by other Christians "because the devil hates and fights the teaching about spiritual gifts."

That is true. Genuine spiritual gifts, functioning in a Christ-adorning manner are devastating to Satan's kingdom.

But that is not the whole truth. Probably half of the opposition to the charismatic movement comes from the Holy Spirit dwelling in the so-called non-charismatics. They sense within that something is very, very wrong among the charismatics.

Finally there are many false gifts because there is a great dearth of the Holy Spirit's gift of discerning of spirits. The church of our Lord, adrift in charismatic confusion, does not know what is what nor who is who. Surely we need to weep.

CHAPTER 14

Afloat on Love

If I had the gift of being able to speak in other languages without learning them, and could speak in every language there is in all of heaven and earth, but didn't love others, I would only be making noise.

If I had the gift of prophecy and knew all about what is going to happen in the future, knew everything about everything, but didn't love others, what good would it do? Even if I had the gift of faith so that I could speak to a mountain and make it move, I would still be worth nothing at all without love.

If I gave everything I have to poor people, and if I were burned alive for preaching the Gospel but didn't love others, it would be of no value whatever.

Love is very patient and kind, never jealous or envious, never boastful or proud.

Never haughty or selfish or rude. Love does not demand its own way. It is not irritable or touchy. It does not hold grudges and will hardly even notice when others do it wrong.

It is never glad about injustice, but rejoices whenever truth wins out.

If you love someone you will be loyal to him no matter what the cost. You will always believe in him, always expect the best of him, and always stand your ground in defending him.

All the special gifts and powers from God will someday come to an end, but love goes on forever. Someday prophecy, and speaking in unknown languages, and special knowledge—these gifts will disappear.

Now we know so little, even with our special gifts, and the preaching of those most gifted is still so poor.

But when we have been made perfect and complete, then the need for these inadequate special gifts will come to an end, and they will disappear.

It's like this: when I was a child I spoke and thought and reasoned as a child does. But when I became a man my thoughts grew far beyond those of my childhood, and now I have put away the childish things.

In the same way, we can see and understand only a little about God now, as if we were peering at his reflection in a poor mirror; but someday we are going to see him in his completeness, face to face. Now all that I know, is hazy and blurred, but then I will see everything clearly, just as clearly as God sees into my heart right now.

There are three things that remain—faith, hope, and love—and the greatest of these is love.
—1 Cor. 13, The Living Bible.

The good Gospel ship is intended to float on love, and Paul makes it abundantly clear in this message which is commonly referred to as the love chapter.

Love distinguished

The first principle is that love is distinct from

any and all of the gifts. Secondly, I must make it clear that if the choice were between love and the gifts (and it shouldn't have to be), the choice would always fall on the side of love.

Love contrasted

In his opening section (vv. 1-3) Paul deliberately contrasts love with the spiritual gifts. Neither tongues, even angelic tongues, nor prophecy, nor the word of knowledge, nor forth telling, nor giving, nor even martyrdom, have any value apart from love.

One of my friends makes this observation about 1 Corinthians 13: "It is interesting to note that after mentioning nine gifts in chapter 12, Paul mentions the word love nine times in chapter 13, contrasting it with the gifts."

Love, St. Paul makes clear, is the lubricating oil by which the spiritual gifts function. Without it, he also emphasizes, spiritual gifts may be abrasive and worthless.

And I think it is not going too far to say that he is directly implying that apostleship or administrating, teaching or healing would also be very unattractive indeed without the fragrance of love clearly manifest. Gifts of revelation operating apart from love can be very problematical. All that God reveals is not necessarily to be told. There are in fact a large number of scriptures which could be cited in support of the "discipline of silence." And surely rushing to announce to someone that he has a demon, even if it is so, is the very thing Paul assails here.

We might proceed through the lists. What value is there in exhortation without love? In healing a man and not caring one whit for his soul, his future, or his present poverty?

Love described

Let us not miss the fact that the description of love at this point is undertaken in the context of a corrective letter to the Corinthian believers. We might well expect Paul to allude and obliquely refer to the spiritual gifts while describing love.

Evidently there had been uncharitable behavior at Corinth, perhaps assembly pride. Love is longsuffering, not envious, not self-promoting and certainly not proud.

Pride, charismatic pride, is the great peril of the specially gifted. Many times when love is absent, the less gifted are called cold and not in tune with the "move" of the Spirit. Insufferable charismatic pride has been all too often the distinctive characteristic of those who claim so much of God's Spirit. Yet nothing more jarring can result than when spiritual gifts and the spirit of pride work together. Surely also, the enemy gets many footholds through charismatic pride because God himself has determined to "resist the proud."

This love "doth not behave itself unseemly." Spiritual gifts and supposed or spurious gifts have stimulated all kinds of erratic behavior. Sometimes the deceiving logic is, "I'll do anything to please the Lord." And more often than not that anything does not adorn the doctrine of Christ. But love adorns.

Love is unselfish. It is easy going; it does not delight to flush evil out into the public eye. It is decorous and modest. It rejoices in the truth, not in what it can do.

Love supersedes

A remarkable change takes place in chapter

13, verse 8. The understanding I get from the passage is that Paul is saying, "Now listen, these gifts are going to finally pass away. They are, after all, the things which accompany spiritual childhood and immaturity. We know in part. We prophesy in part. The day will come when these pretty jewels will be put aside. We still look at this subject through tinted glasses, but one day when Christ comes it will be face to face. Spiritual gifts are necessary for now, but don't make a big thing out of them."

Let me interject a personal word here. Earlier in these pages I suggested that spiritual gifts do not make one spiritual. And though I have seen the teaching in other parts of the Scriptures, I do not know how many times I had read 1 Corinthians 13 without seeing this thought. But I have discovered now and have seen for the first time in this writing that Paul was gently saying much the same thing here. Spiritual growth and maturity will certainly involve manifestation of the spiritual gifts, but preoccupation with gifts is not only unwholesome Christianity; it produces distortion in personal Christian growth and trouble for the church.

The summary

But does this cautious corrective mood mean that spiritual gifts are to be dismissed or ignored? Far from it. In 13:13 and 14:1 the emphasis is clear:

> And now abideth faith, hope, charity, these three; but the greatest of these is charity. ... Follow after charity, and desire spiritual gifts, but rather that ye may prophesy.

Follow after love and desire spiritual gifts.

You need both. It's like the two tracks of the railroad. Tear up one track and you will wreck the train.

Or to change the figure, love is like a wide river and the gifts are like the little boats that float upon it. Boats without a river are grotesque and tilted. But the wide river without boats is still majestic in itself. Ideally, though, the boats are there upon the river's broad expanse.

"Follow after love." It is something one does, seeks, pursues. And desire spiritual gifts. That, too, is something to be done: "Covet earnestly the best gifts."

From personal experience I would say that should one separate three days for fasting and prayer to seek a revelation of God's love or a manifestation of His gifts or both, that person would be pleasantly surprised at the response of our loving Lord.

It is a deep pain to me that the polarization and separation among evangelicals on the spiritual gifts has produced in most cases either a harsh denunciation of all that is supernatural or an unhealthy fixation upon one miraculous gift.

Our Lord intended a beautiful balance. And something within me cries that once again it should be so.

AUTHOR'S NOTE

Some of the material that immediately follows is, for want of a better word, heavy. But it is necessary and part of a complete thought. Therefore consider the next three chapters as part of a whole. Please do not lift one chapter out of its total context. If you can possibly read all three chapters at one sitting, it will contribute greatly to the balanced view I seek to present. Necessarily, I use some negative illustrations but even these should be weighed against the positive emphasis of earlier and later chapters.

CHAPTER 15

Tests for Tongues

On one occasion in Guatemala I was preaching in a conference where one group of young people was isolating itself and speaking in tongues. Whenever the young people talked with me, I kept insisting that they keep things in biblical order (see chapter 12).

But their excitement made them very difficult to restrain, and the tensions on both sides
of a divided conference made the preaching difficult.

On the final Sunday, the afternoon ministry
of the missionary speaker was especially blessed
—but the tongues-speaking teenagers were not
there. I learned later that they were out on a
hillside practicing their gifts.

When one of the fellows came to me later,
he was breathless with excitement. I asked him
where they had gone and what had happened
and why they had not been in the scheduled
service.

"Well," he said, "we went out and had a
service of our own."

"How many spoke in tongues?" I asked, and
he knew by my question that I wanted to know
if they had gone beyond the biblical limit of
three.

"Three spoke in tongues," he said, "but then
some more girls came." I gathered that more
tongues-speaking had taken place.

Then I asked, "What was the message given
through the tongues?" He looked at me a bit
sheepishly and replied, "The message was,
'What are you kids doing out here? Why aren't
you in the meeting?' "

What must one conclude from an incident
like that? Can one conclude anything? Surely
God must grant His church wisdom and discernment. I still have not drawn any clear conclusion about the incident I have related above.
Because there was no opportunity to apply the
tests we are discussing here, I remain uncertain,
doubtful. Are you surprised that I do not immediately accept such an incident as prompted
by the Holy Spirit? Read on.

There are scriptural tests which can be applied to tongues and prophecy and the other less abused spiritual gifts. And with these scriptural tests we are able to be discerning, even in the most amazing and confusing circumstances.

The biblical tests

Does the tongue or other manifestation measure up to Paul's corrective passage in 1 Corinthians 12, 13 and 14? If the biblical order is ignored, for example, by everyone speaking in tongues at once, by tongues without interpretation, or by more than three speaking in tongues, then the manifestation is out of order biblically. Other examples could be cited. Disregard for biblical order is probably the easiest aberration to detect—and correct.

The practical tests

There are times when the discerning child of God may witness manifestations that are apparently in biblical order but still something appears to be wrong.

The question to ask then is, "Does this manifestation adorn the doctrine of Jesus Christ?" The Holy Spirit, we may be sure, will always desire to do so.

A second question: Is pride involved here? Such pride was the curse of the Corinthian church, and today it readily reappears when the emphasis on Christian love diminishes. Charismatic pride is consistently stimulated by erroneous teaching which leads new or immature Christians to believe they have attained great spiritual heights because spiritual gifts are manifested.

A third question: Is the result of the manifestation divisive? The Holy Spirit struggles always to maintain the harmony of the local congregation of believers, but a divisive spirit is not from God. (An exception to this general rule should be noted: When spiritual renewal is experienced by part of a congregation and opposed by another part, division may ultimately be forced by those who reject renewal.)

A fourth question: Is there order? Paul's instruction was certainly clear enough, "Let everything be done decently and in order" (1 Cor. 14:40). He also said, "God is not the author of confusion" (1 Cor. 14:33).

Charismatic testing

The discerning of spirits, as we have already noted, is one of the gifts of the Holy Spirit so sorely needed in our day. Since speaking in tongues is a spiritual manifestation and involves spirit-speaking, the discerning of spirits is one of the means God uses, enabling earnest Christians to distinguish between the true and the false. Discerning of spirits is part of the protection Christ has given to His church, no doubt because it is continually under attack. Indeed, there will be many occasions when the function of the gift of discerning of spirits will be all that is needed to determine the source and inspiration of a spiritual manifestation.

That the church is lacking this gift seems painfully obvious. Some believers, on the one side, vigorously assert that there just never are false tongues. Others, at the other end of the spectrum, are certain that all utterance manifestations are demonic and never from the Holy Spirit. A functioning gift of the discerning of spirits, in my view, would considerably temper both attitudes.

Nevertheless, a complete reliance upon discerning of spirits is not really wise. And there are reasons why this is so. If it exists in an atmosphere where it is psychologically impossible to admit the possibility of spurious gifts, no false manifestations will ever be detected. There are charismatic Christians who apparently have excellent deliverance ministries but have never encountered false charismatic manifestations.

Also, since discerning of spirits is subjective; that is, someone is going to say "This is of God," or "That is not of God," there is always the possibility that subjective impressions will take precedence over biblical tests.

Also, discerning of spirits will not be available in every situation. Since it is a charismatic manifestation that God sovereignly distributes in His will, only some of God's children will have it. Were it a universal characteristic of all Christians, or even all groups of God's children, the need for the other tests we mention here would be considerably reduced.

Apparently, also, it is not a gift that can be operated at will. It seems that the Holy Spirit wants to use His children, not be used of them.

So we are saying, thank God for discerning of spirits. It is a valid part of the Christian arsenal. But it is not intended to be the only resource for believers who wish to *prove all things.*

Theological tests

Nothing should be received which is not correct doctrinally, especially with tongues and prophecy, but with other manifestations as well. If, as is often the case, the Trinity is denied, dates are set for Christ's return, or small groups retire to isolated places to await the tribulation, there can be no doubt that the tongues and prophecy are false. False prophecies, under the guise of false purity, also tend to seek to sever the sexual relationships of marriage. Mature Christians with a good knowledge of the Word will not likely have any difficulty in detecting prophecy or tongues that are false theologically. New or weak Christians may be victimized. Most often, the victims have motives without reproach; they want only all that God has. But they are deceived.

Another question to ask, Does this manifestation glorify Christ and draw attention to His person, or does it focus attention elsewhere? The Scriptures teach that the Holy Spirit does not speak of himself (John 16:13) but glorifies Christ (14). The Christian who becomes a Holy Spirit or charismatic "buff" is following a deflected compass.

The love test

For a considerable period of time I felt that the ultimate test for any spiritual operation was the love test. I still feel that way if the love manifested is genuine. But sadly I have come to learn that there is a spurious love as well as the real. In *A Revolution of Love* I wrote about what I have every reason to believe was the genuine love of the Holy Spirit. But later, in an overseas trip, I was confronted with false love. The words and actions were proper but the spirit was wrong. I found myself wanting to run out of the church in which divine love was being prostituted.

The key, I feel, to a true manifestation of

God's love among Christians is that the love must spring from a "pure heart, and of a good conscience, and of faith unfeigned" (1 Tim. 1:5). "The Love of God is shed abroad in our hearts by the Holy Spirit" (Rom. 5:5).

Where attempts are made to experience, demonstrate or show God's love apart from obedience and holiness, the results are certain to be unhappy.

Sadly, too, I have come to the conclusion that joyful and radiant countenances are not always reliable evidences of what is of God. People can have great experiences and look as though they have swallowed light bulbs but still have a false gift. The enemy of our souls is an angel of light, and we forget it at our own peril.

Love, then, which springs from holiness of life, which is demonstratively of God and results in obedience to God, is another indication that a spiritual gift may be genuine.

Love can be imitated, can be false, and for that reason is not the last test in my list.

Spiritual tests

The Bible describes these spiritual tests in the following passages:

> Wherefore I give you to understand, that no man speaking by the Spirit of God calleth Jesus accursed: and that no man can say that Jesus is the Lord, but by the Holy Ghost. —1 Cor. 12:3.
> Despise not prophesyings.
> Prove all things; hold fast that which is good.—1 Thess. 5:20, 21.
> Beloved, believe not every spirit, but try the spirits whether they are of God: because

many false prophets are gone out into the world.

Hereby know ye the Spirit of God: Every spirit that confesseth that Jesus Christ is come in the flesh is of God:

And every spirit that confesseth not that Jesus Christ is come in the flesh is not of God: and this is that spirit of antichrist, whereof ye have heard that it should come; and even now already is it in the world.—1 John 4:1-3.

The spirits are to be tried, and I have come to the conclusion that this means far more than just to examine the utterance in biblical, practical, theological and charismatic ways.

John does not say we should try the prophet or what the prophet says. John says, "Try the spirits."

Every spirit that continually *says* "Jesus Christ is come in the flesh" is of God. Silence on that, refusal to answer, reluctant admission, or an open denial of that fact—all demonstrate that the spirit is not of God. It was particularly enlightening to me to realize finally that *grudging or deceptive admission, silence and denial are all proofs that the spirit is not of God.*

One of the greatest pains I have suffered in the ministry was to have a dear friend who had been deceived by a false prophet listen carefully to my exhortation to leave the man. I had withheld my exhortation for months and when I finally shared, I sensed that my words were exploding in his heart.

Then he began to speak in tongues because he wanted to know whether or not it was of God. It was rough and abrasive. He said, "What do you think, Neill?" I didn't know.

The truths I am sharing here about testing tongues were clarified later. But if ever my friend was ready to forsake the prophet it was then. Lack of knowledge on my part was so very costly because he could have been freed that day.

The spirit that is of God, whether manifesting in tongues or prophecy, must invariably and repeatedly confess that Jesus Christ is come in the flesh. To confess means to say.

In testing utterances it is important to distinguish between the person and the spirit manifesting. The Christian worker should make it clear to the person involved that he is addressing the spirit and not the individual.

It goes nearly without saying that the person who wishes to have a manifestation tested must be completely cooperative with the one who applies the test. The individual should clearly understand that he as a person is not to respond.

If, for example, testing is forced upon unwilling tongues-speakers, the result may be confusing.

On one occasion a pastor friend came to me asking for assistance. He had two young fellows preaching in his church, one of whom he knew spoke in tongues, and he was uneasy about their ministry. He wanted the test to be applied.

We discovered that they both spoke in tongues, but they of course were not anxious to be found false prophets. We applied the test to both, but we were unsatisfied with the results. It appeared that the fellows spoke in tongues, switched off the manifestation to answer positively to the question, "Did Jesus Christ come in the flesh?" and then shifted back into their tongues. I realize now that we found out only if the fellows believed that Jesus Christ came in the flesh. We did not succeed in trying the spirits at all. But the experience was not wasted; we learned what not to do.

The manifestation must be allowed unhindered and uninterrupted expression while the test is being made, and no effort must be made by the person involved to supply the "right" answer.

The repetition of the question, "You spirit now manifesting, is Jesus Christ come in the flesh?" may be important. I have come to expect a spontaneous affirmative answer when the tongues manifestation is genuinely of the Holy Spirit, especially when the test question is put several times.

If the enemy is involved, repetitious questioning (like repetitious commanding, Mark 5:8, Amplified New Testament) will often shake the enemy loose and provoke abrasive or antagonistic reactions—and of course clarify the case.

Sometimes the spirit may respond with a positive answer that is at the same time equivocative and/or evasive. For example, a spirit might respond, "Of course I believe in Jesus." But *which* Jesus is not specified. If there is any hint of subterfuge, stick to the biblical test. Repeat it. Enlarge upon it by requiring answers to such questions as these: Is Jesus Christ Lord? Is Jesus Christ anathema? Does all the fullness of the Godhead dwell bodily in Jesus Christ? This procedure is likely to clarify the issue fully.

In 1 John 4:2 and 3 the verb forms used indicate that every spirit that *continually and genuinely* confesses that Jesus Christ is come in the flesh is of God. Therefore reluctant admissions or occasional positive declarations that Jesus Christ is come in the flesh are not sufficient. *The confession must be continual. A superficial understanding of this principle can short circuit the whole procedure of testing.*

(Demons can and do lie. Thus, the words *continually* and *genuinely* in the paragraph above are of utmost importance. Also, as we have just noted, the Greek verbs used in 1 Corinthians 12:3 and 1 John 4:2 and 3 do come down strongly on the continuous idea.)

Illustrations of deceitful positive affirmations are not hard to come by. In the Dominican Republic I met a Christian woman who habitually twitched and shuddered in prayer meetings. She had a tongues manifestation which seemed to take over when she wanted to praise the Lord. But when the manifestation was confronted, the confession of Jesus Christ, though positive, was accented, even faintly humorous or mocking, and in English which the woman definitely did not know. I believe in retrospect that it was a false confession.

A friend who wrote to me during the writing of this book related an incident where invading spirits named one of their co-inhabitors, "Jesus." So of course they all knew and loved "Jesus." The spirits had to be confronted with "which Jesus?"

Another friend added yet another illustration. In the process of a deliverance a spirit claiming to be the Holy Spirit manifested itself in the victim. All tests were applied with positive results. When my friend returned home from a trip, he found his colleagues persuaded that the Holy Spirit indeed had taken control of the person. All he had to follow was a discerning witness that something was wrong. He initiated a confrontation and the phony "Holy Spirit" was uncovered.

Thus, as we have said elsewhere in these

pages, there are *four possibilities* with spirit-testing: (1) a positive affirmation which is genuine and continual, (2) a positive affirmation which is not continual but is intended to deceive, (3) a denial, and (4) silence. 1 John 4:2 and 3 lays a four-sided trap for the enemy, and the Christian worker must know where the biblical lines are drawn.

There is also the possibility of inner responses, both negative and positive. In such a case the willingness and absolute cooperation of the person involved is vital. He or she will know what the inner response is and be able to pass it on to the Christian worker conducting the test.

The material we include here is definitely for the use of mature Christians, pastors and elders. And anyone who might take this material as authorization for a belligerent ministry of "tongues-testing" would be very foolish.

And nowhere is the exhortation to let everything be established in the mouth of two or three witnesses more pertinent than here. The pastor or Christian worker who has one or two discerning elders who can assist him in trying the spirits is fortunate indeed.

If a pastor observes doubtful manifestations in his congregation, as a shepherd of the flock, I feel personally he has every right to ask to be permitted to test the manifestation. But he should be ready for the fireworks and to proceed with exorcism in the event of false manifestations. He should also be prepared to instruct the inquiring person if the manifestation proves fleshly. If the person himself is creating the "tongue" and no spiritual manifestation is involved, it may be judged fleshly.

Also, before the test is applied, one should prepare the person involved for the possibility that there has been deception. To admit that one has been deceived is a very high hurdle indeed.

CHAPTER 16

This Is What Happens

At this juncture I wish to narrate several experiences; the first took place in 1963 and the others more recently.

I believe my readers all realize after getting this far into the book that I most certainly believe that there are true manifestations of the Holy Spirit. Three of these illustrations are cases where the spirit has *not* been of God.

Some years ago a teenager in deep spiritual trouble came to us. It soon became evident that her case was one of severe demonic invasion, and the deliverance covered a period of seven months. She received a great deliverance and was a radiant Christian for years afterward.

But about six weeks into the deliverance, which included many all-night sessions and long struggles against the enemy, the girl suddenly began to sing in tongues. The melody was very beautiful. We believed it certainly to be a divine tongue. But she had been and still was a demonized girl. So we carefully tested the spirit.

We used the same procedures we had used with non tongues-speaking spirits.

We said something like this: "You spirit that is now manifesting, did Jesus Christ come in the flesh?" There was an instant reply in the middle of the unknown words and beautiful melody. It was the English word "Yes." The spirit was tried repeatedly with the same result.

However, the girl remained under demonic control for several months after that. During the time of her bondage the only time she could confess that Jesus Christ had come in the flesh was when she was singing in tongues. Apart from the tongues, we would say to the girl, "Did Jesus come in the flesh?" She wanted to say yes, but since the demons still controlled her, they seized her vocal chords and she was unable to confess the lordship of Jesus apart from tongues. This condition continued for a period of time after the experience I have now related.

I believe that to draw theological implications from a single experience would be unwise. But I do feel that this case stands as a clear-cut illustration of trying the spirits and of a genuine tongue.

Before I go further with these examples, I must insert here that I am fully aware that this may prove unsettling to many. In fact, I have been deeply burdened. I want this to be a loving, compassionate book, but the tendency of some may be to assume that I am being unnecessarily negative. Yet I have filled chapters with the positive and beautiful truths about spiritual gifts. They are beautiful. They are for us today. Thank God.

At the same time a vast deception has been foisted upon God's dear children. And there is just no painless way to say what I have been saying and what I must still say. My problem with negative illustrations is not to find them, but to keep from filling chapter after chapter with them.

I know especially that some of my Pentecostal brethren will be upset when I suggest at all that tongues should be tested. One author quotes a letter written by a charismatic Christian to a friend of his.

The Christian was concerned because the Evangelical Ministers' Association had brought a man to their community for a week-long seminar and the visiting minister not only taught the necessity of testing tongues but narrated incidents in which demonic tongues had been cast out and the ability to speak in tongues had been lost. The concerned Christian was losing sleep over such events and wanted an answer.

The charismatic response, if I may take the eloquence of the writer under discussion as typical, is unsettling. He says only that the visiting minister had never been baptized with the Holy Spirit and that he was attempting to discredit the genuine spiritual experience of the baptism with the Holy Spirit.

It is not enough to say that the evangelical minister was against the baptism with the Holy Spirit and speaking in tongues. He may have been. But that does not by any means signify that all who feel testing the spirits (including tongues) is necessary, are anticharismatic. And the author in question skirts the issue of trying the spirits altogether.

"Believe not every spirit." The command is to avoid naivete and gullibility, "But try the spirits whether they are of God." I do not think this scripture is warrant to send one on a "tongues-testing" mission. But it is a warning all the same.

John says not to believe "every spirit." And he says "try the spirits." The word *every* is missing in the second phrase. Discrimination between the true and false can be made by other tests as described in the last chapter. The final court of appeal is to try the spirit. *All spiritual manifestations without exception are to be questioned. Some spirits are to be tried.*

And though there be lying spirits by the thousands, two things circumscribe them. First, they cannot and will not ever continually and genuinely confess that Jesus Christ is Lord (1 Cor. 12:3). Secondly, they steadfastly refuse to continually and genuinely confess that Jesus Christ is come in the flesh, *sometimes they retreat to silence, but even the silence betrays the evil spirits.* John makes it clear, "Every spirit that confesseth not that Jesus Christ is come in the flesh is not of God" (1 John 4:2).

Experience, of course, is not a fit base for biblical doctrine, but when doctrine is confirmed by experience, then those who differ must listen very carefully to what is said. And I want so much to say it compassionately.

Now to the second example. Recently a lovely Christian girl came to me asking, "Would you test my tongues?" I agreed to do so, but delays kept us from it until the final day of one of our summer conventions.

She had never spoken the words of the tongue aloud, but they had been running through her mind at intervals since she had attended a charismatic meeting in Calgary, Alberta, and had received the laying on of hands there.

I instructed her to speak the words of the tongue aloud, and I knelt beside her and began to speak repeatedly in the following manner, "You spirit that is now manifesting, did Jesus Christ come in the flesh?" Soon she stopped me. "I feel a big 'no' forming in my mind. I don't think that this is of God," she said.

So we simply made a verbal commitment in which she said something like this, "I here and now refuse, reject and repudiate completely this spirit of false tongues. I take back all the ground I have ever given to the devil, knowingly or unknowingly, and I give it to the Lord Jesus Christ. This I do in Jesus' name."

The next day she greeted me with a radiant smile. "It's gone."

The third illustration in one sense sprang from the second. The young lady evidently said something about what had happened to her. Several intermediate events followed, and finally a teenager, along with her girl friend, visited our home.

My wife entered into a lengthy counselling ministry with the troubled teenager. Then at 2:30 a.m. my wife wakened me and asked me to join the counselling session. At about 4:30 a.m. the girl was kneeling upright on our living room rug and speaking in tongues which we believed to be spurious. We commanded something like this, "You spirit that is now manifesting, in the name of Jesus Christ, the Son of God who came in the flesh, we command you to interpret and speak in English."

The command was instantly obeyed. The words were "I am the Lord of all, I am the devil." Unfortunately, deliverance did not come because the girl persisted in an unhealthy curiosity about the supernatural.

The psychic contamination had taken place among what are loosely called the "Jesus People." This illustration should not be construed as a total denunciation of the Jesus generation. One of the major points of this book is that erroneous teaching on tongues opens the door to the enemy and breeds the unhappy mix of true and false so common within the charismatic movement.

A fourth illustration involves a teenage boy. After a Sunday school class in which this subject was touched, he came asking that his tongue be tested. I didn't know that he spoke in tongues but my first reaction was, "Fine. This should be a good tongue. He is such a fine and openhearted Christian."

But as soon as he began to speak in tongues the spirit seized his face and contorted it. Persistently the question was put, "You spirit that is now manifesting, did Jesus Christ come in the flesh?" And the answer came: "No. No." Two spirits of false tongues then had to be dislodged.

The contamination in this case had come from a youth retreat of what we would certainly call a fundamental no-nonsense Pentecostal denomination.

Not for a moment am I suggesting that all of the tongues in that group are false, but apparently some of them are. The error in the matter of tongues opens the door to the mixture which does such great harm to our Lord's church.

John's exhortation is clear enough:

> Beloved, believe not every spirit, but try the spirits whether they are of God: because many false prophets are gone out into the world.
> Hereby know ye the Spirit of God: Every

spirit that confesseth that Jesus Christ is come in the flesh is of God:

And every spirit that confesseth not that Jesus Christ is come in the flesh is not of God: and this is that spirit of antichrist, whereof ye have heard that it should come; and even now already is it in the world.—1 John 4:1-3.

Surely, brethren, the time has come to take these words very, very seriously.

CHAPTER 17

Blasting the Gloom Cloud

Do you remember that I asked you to read these three chapters together? Here is my reason. As necessary as is everything I have already said, there is also something else to be said.

I, for one, cannot imagine a tongues-testing session after the day of Pentecost. The disciples had no previous experience with tongues, but they knew the Holy Spirit had come upon them. Later, however, Satan began his counter-attack upon the infant church, and Paul's Corinthian remarks were addressed to a church which had evidently heard some spirit-speaking where Jesus Christ was not proclaimed as Lord (1 Cor. 12:3). Later still, John talked carefully about trying the spirits, making sure that every spirit manifestation continually confesses that Jesus Christ is come in the flesh (1 John 4:2, 3).

Apparently, then, there is some space between charismatic manifestations and the application of the verbal test.

Or to put it another way, there should be no rush to confrontation with supposedly spurious manifestations. At the same time, the final court of appeal, the acid test, is to try the spirits.

Perhaps an example will illustrate what I am saying. After I had shared the material of the last two chapters in one of our summer conventions, a woman came to me. She was under the gloom cloud and she confirmed it by her words. "What you have said really upsets me."

From our previous conversation I knew she was wondering if her experience of speaking in tongues was genuine. So I asked her a few questions (based on chapter 15). Did this experience in your life ever cause you to behave in an unbiblical way? Did this experience ever cause you to do anything that would not adorn the doctrine of Jesus Christ? Has any interpretation been unsound scripturally, doctrinally, theologically? In each case her answer was a firm *no*. Further, she explained that her charismatic experience had immensely increased her love for the Lord Jesus. Nor did her countenance betray any bondage at all.

"Sister," I said, "I'm satisfied that your experience of speaking in tongues is from the Holy Spirit. If there is any lingering doubt in your mind, we can always apply the verbal test, but I don't see that it is necessary."

She was understandably relieved, and out she came from under the gloom cloud. And I learned something very important. This material, unless held in careful perspective, could in certain cases bring sincere Spirit-filled Christians under the gloom cloud. To avoid that eventuality, I have written this chapter and earnestly ask you to consider it one with the other two. I don't want to give the enemy a peg to hang anything over anybody.

At the same time I'm surely not in favor of letting the phony stuff get by. The mother whose case I have just discussed above had introduced her son-in-law to speaking in tongues. One of my friends would say she "hustled" him for tongues and "laid the tongues trip" on him. But when I talked to her she regretted her action because following the charismatic experience her son-in-law's spiritual life had fallen to a dismal low. In my mind, her son-in-law has a tongues manifestation which sorely needs to be tested.

Am I making myself clear? I'm saying that we must do away with credulity and gullibility. We must stop accepting everything supernatural as from God Almighty just because it happens in church. We have been naive for too long.

I'm also saying that testing tongues is not necessarily the first reaction we should have to a manifestation. A questioning spirit? Yes. But a rush to judgment? No. Let the verbal test remain as a final court of appeal for cases that are not clarified by other means. But the Bible speaks about trying the spirits. God knew there would be times when we would need it. And believe me, it wouldn't be in the Bible if we didn't need it.

I know that many believers who have an experience in tongues are going to read this book. Let me speak to you for a moment. If the devil tries to cover you with the gloom cloud, a few simple questions can blast it away.

Do you struggle with depression, fear, uncontrollable emotion or illicit sexual urges? Are you really free in Jesus Christ? You may not relate your spiritual problems with speaking in tongues at all, when in fact that experience, if spurious, can be the open door to all kinds of spiritual enslavement.

Do you ever have an uneasy feeling about the source of your experience?

Does the manifestation in your life ever prompt unbiblical behavior?

Does the manifestation in your life ever cause you to do things that are erratic, that do not adorn the doctrine of Christ?

Does the manifestation carry with it interpretations which are faulty doctrinally or theologically?

Does the manifestation deepen your love for the Lord Jesus Christ and His Word?

In many cases, just answering those questions will resolve the issue and sweep away the gloom cloud. But if not, read on.

The gloom cloud may well hover over the intersection where biblical truth and spurious experience have collided. For example, in a certain hospital room there was a lady who always switched to another TV channel when Billy Graham came on. Her reason? He made her depressed.

I know very well (and I say this carefully) that many of my readers are going to discover, if they have not suspected it earlier, that they have been deceived by a spurious charismatic experience. The next chapter will be especially helpful, but right now my word to you is this: Go to war against the enemy. Determine to renounce and repudiate Satan completely. And under no condition allow a spiritual manifestation in your person which does not continually, willingly genuinely and joyfully confess that Jesus Christ is Lord and that He is come in the flesh. If necessary, have the spirit tested. And if it is false, by all means get rid of it. That will blast the gloom cloud too.

CHAPTER 18

Facing Deception

If what I am recording here gets wide circulation, thousands of sincere Christians are going to call in question a spiritual experience they have had, some perhaps for years. The repercussions could be immense.

Another thing is certain to happen: This book will be read by some about to be captivated by the pseudo-charismatic. In such cases what is being reported here will serve as a much needed brake.

I wish to make it clear that I am totally in favor of all that the Holy Spirit of Almighty God has done and wishes to do. But I am unalterably opposed to what Satan has done or wishes to do.

Moreover, in the Word of God there are serious warnings to those who cause others to doubt. And there is a very fine line between the sowing of doubt and the spiritual discernment which we seek above all else in this present writing.

Some will feel a great uneasiness when they read these remarks. I passed this manuscript around enough to find that out. But don't be too quick to blame the book. If what I am saying is biblical, then the uncertainty may be no more than the obvious result of biblical truth coming against deception. The solution is not to throw the book aside; the solution is to try the spirits, to clarify the case, and to face deception if necessary.

But now—how to face deception.

First, the possibility of deception must be recognized as a pervasive current through all of Scripture from the subtlety of the Deceiver in the garden to the witnessing of the False Prophet in Revelation; the patterns are regular and the warnings consistent.

Every man must face the fact that on occasion he has been deceived. To ignore that possibility is nigh inexplicable gullibility.

Frequently in charismatic deception, a dangerous thought pattern will emerge which rationalizes thus: "This must be of God because . . ." Most times the reason given will be based upon feelings or experience at the expense of what is biblical.

Sometimes, many times, an appeal is made to providential circumstances and miraculous events to prove that the Holy Spirit is at work. Though the devil has a hard time getting away with twisting the scriptures, we fall for his false "providences" nearly every time. When Jonah, the rebellious prophet, was running away from God, he found a boat at the right time and the right place ready to receive him. He might have said, "Jehovah is with me. I must not be running away from God at all. Look at how this has all worked out." All too often "providential" circumstances are part of the deception.

In my view there is only one thing worse than being deceived. And that is to be deceived and never know it.

Deception in the area of spiritual gifts, especially speaking in tongues, is very difficult to face. "Is this gift, which I have always considered to be a mark of spirituality and a sign of the baptism of the Holy Spirit, no more than a master deception? If I have been deceived here, where else have I been deceived?"

The latter question is possibly more difficult to face than the first, but they are both very uncomfortable queries, though necessary all the same.

A first reaction to all of this may be anger. Who is this man who writes this way? What right does he have to question speaking in tongues? If I question my tongues, I will be doubting God.

The right, even obligation, to question spiritual manifestations is a biblical one: "Prove all things," "Believe not every spirit." These exhortations are given in a context relating to utterance gifts and spirit-speaking.

Protesting the views expounded here may be an unhealthy sign. *The deception you preserve may be your own. After all, the Holy Spirit has absolutely nothing to fear from biblical tests and standards.* He is the one who inspired the Scriptures.

Some will protest that anyone with a true gift of discerning of spirits will be able to tell which spiritual manifestations are true and which are false. That is partially true, but not the whole truth. Not everyone is going to have discerning of spirits. And the danger is that a subjective experience ("God has revealed to me that this tongue is genuine") could take the place of the various biblical tests. It is a dangerous path, vulnerable to deception on a second level to cover for the first.

Also, when false tongues, for example, have been confronted and dislodged, the enemy does not give up. The person who has been liberated from false manifestations but is still not completely free from occult subjection will face an unprecedented satanic campaign designed to regain the lost ground. The only resource in such cases is to take an adamant, verbal, audible stand against the devil and in favor of Almighty God.

Terminology is important. Use the full title of the Lord Jesus Christ, because there are many *antichrists* in the world. At one of our conventions a sister who was in the process of being delivered was taken by a spirit which said repeatedly, "Jesus, Jesus, Jesus." Unfortunately the "Jesus" was not the Lord Jesus Christ. The spirit was dislodged in His name.

It may ultimately be necessary to seek out a non-charismatic or "third view" deliverance ministry. Around the world there is a growing corps of God's servants who will vouch for much of the contents of this book biblically and on the basis of their own experiences. They have also learned how to help the deceived escape from the psuedo-charismatic. A wise pastor or a trusted friend may be the one God will use to help you.

The following testimony will be of immense help to any who have been deceived. I know the circumstances personally, and the experience was indeed a lesson learned at a great cost. Though the deception was not on the point of tongues, it could be classified as a charismatic deception. Please read carefully the remainder of this chapter as another person shares.

The Dark Hole of Deception
(by one who has been there)

Deception! What an ugly word! Yet the Scriptures make it very clear that Satan will sharpen this particular aspect of his working in the time immediately preceding Christ's return. Deception will be his chief weapon, and it will be " . . . planned to beguile men at every stage of life; (1) deception of the unregenerate who are already deceived by sin; (2) deception suited to the carnal Christian; (3) and deception fitted to the spiritual believer, who has passed out of the preceding stages into a realm where he will be open to meet more subtle wiles." [1]

Earlier recognition and acceptance of the last part of that statement could have saved this writer much turmoil of mind and spirit. This article is an effort to emphasize the fact that Satan has special forces out to deceive those who wholly want to live for God and who have experienced the filling of the Spirit and endeavor to walk daily in His power and love.

Some will no doubt question how such a one could possibly be deceived. Let it suffice to say unequivocally that it *is* possible for an earnest believer to find himself in this position. But let it be said, too, that no matter what damage Satan can inflict, God is over all, glorious, victorious, and there is *always* hope.

The very word deception indicates that an untruth is made to be credible, and it begins when the devil can so construe the facts in a person's mind as to cause him to believe the lie. The chief areas of his attack are in doctrine, spiritual experience, and moral conduct. Never does Satan make his lies so outrageous as to be incredible. They will be made-to-order for each indiviual temperament and personality.

Once the first lie is accepted, further evidences, truths, circumstances, and quotations are all readily available to deepen the deception. All this is looked upon to be sincere and pure, and therein lies the subtlety of deception.

Let me repeat, my purpose here is twofold: to emphasize that it is possible to be deceived at any level of spiritual maturity and to give some helpful suggestions to those who may find themselves in deception.

Thank God, He is faithful and merciful and if a person is sensitive to His dealings, God will bring across his path people, circumstances, and even an increasing sense of restraint in one's own spirit which will hopefully put at least a question mark in the mind and lead to the following actions:

1. *Admitting the possibility of being deceived.* One can be sure that Satan will fight "tooth and nail" to hinder even this step because it truly is the beginning of his downfall. His lies will be many and varied: "You are committing the sin of unbelief by questioning God." "You must keep on believing, for all things are possible." "You are grieving the Holy Spirit and opposing God's will for your life." "You are committing the unpardonable sin."

At this point one should remember that Satan is not only the arch-deceiver but the father of lies and that the scripture exhorts us to "prove all things" and to "try the spirits." Honest "doubting" is always acceptable to God. As the possibility of deception is contemplated, God will shed His light on the situation until the refuge of lies will be gone and one admits the deception.

2. *Voicing the admission: "I have been deceived."* One of the greatest stumbling blocks to this step is just plain old "self"—pride. The person will want to maintain the position that has been assumed, and Satan may even be able to get the believer to side with him in defense of the deception.

Actually to admit to being deceived is a most devastating experience. The whole basis of spiritual experience suddenly lies shattered. Satan will be sure to have it questioned thus, "Well, if that is a deception, then what is true?" It is best during this time not to make any judgments on past experiences. Undoubtedly there has been true, God-given spiritual experience mixed with the false, but at this point one should hold in abeyance all judgments.

Thoughts that are absolutely repulsive will come to the mind: "God failed you. He said you could believe His Word and now He has let you down. How can you love a God like that?" Satan will also tell you that never again will your discernment be reliable, that you cannot trust your own judgment on anything, that any stability of character you may have possessed is now completely gone, and that someday you may even end up in a mental institution.

3. *Exercising the will.* Some point of reference must be established, and for the Christian it is God's Word.

The emphasis here is on the will. The mind will be in utter confusion and the emotions weak and seemingly lifeless. Several declarations of the will should be made: "I believe the Bible to be the infallible Word of God. It is absolute truth and I will believe whatever it says." In answer to the devil's persistent lies say (out loud if possible), "Jesus Christ never fails, God is faithful, and what He says He will do. God is love and His mercy endures forever." Such affirmations will strengthen faith and give courage.

Private devotions and worship will likely be almost nonexistent, but the following declaration should be made: "Almighty God, whatever your will is, I want it. Satan, whatever your will is, I refuse and repudiate it."

4. *Launching an all-out war for God, against Satan.* One can affirm his position by immediately determining to fight the enemy. The person should determine that he wants to get to the basis of whatever caused the problem and made him susceptible to the very first lie. Total honesty with oneself and with God will be necessary no matter how painful the process may become. God promises to forgive our sins if we will confess them. They must be identified. The Holy Spirit will bring light to the mind regarding this, and terms will come that exactly describe the problem. This process should be recognized as the mercy and love of God showing the way to freedom and should be accepted with deep gratitude.

The more precisely the sins are named the greater the deliverance will be. The basic sins of believing the lie of the devil as well as failure to judge all things according to Scripture should be confessed. The believer should also take back any ground that he knowingly or unknowingly gave to the enemy and by an act of his will give it to God.

The following commitment should be made with each individual problem as it is brought to the surface by the light of God's Word and the conviction of the Holy Spirit: "Almighty God, in the name of the Lord Jesus Christ and by His blood, I now refuse, renounce, and repudiate this spirit of _____ and I cast it into the abyss. Holy Spirit of God, I ask you to occupy that area of my life."

It may be that a person has wrongfully put himself knowingly or unknowingly under the subjection of some human being. This can be dealt with by confessing " . . . my unlawful subjection to (name of individual). I place myself under subjection only to Almighty God" (and for women, to their own husbands).

Through the process of time the spirit of the believer will gradually become freer to praise, pray, and worship. One should be careful not to let the devil rob him of all past blessings but should seek to ground his experience and practice firmly on the written Word of God and to meet the devil's accusations with "Thus saith the Lord." The Psalms will be of great encouragement as one will readily identify with the heart-cry of David expressed in so many of them.

5. *Purposing to live totally for God and others.* The tendency will be to withdraw from Christian fellowship because "I don't trust myself anymore." I thank God that in my own experience during those dark days I was forced by circumstances to be with people and to carry on the normal routine of life. In God's great love and mercy He will turn even such a bitter experience for the good if we allow Him to do so.

True, the hole of deception is dark and deep, but not hopeless. Praise God, there is deliverance. Just reach up and touch Him. He is there!

CHAPTER 19

The Gentle Maybe

A "third view"?

A "gentle maybe"?

What do I mean? Essentially, I am saying that in the discussion of spiritual gifts the emphasis must return to Hebrews 2:4 and 1 Corinthians 12:11. "God also bearing them witness, both with signs and wonders, and with divers miracles, and gifts of the Holy Ghost, *according to his own will.*" "But all these worketh that one and the selfsame Spirit, dividing to every man severally *as he will.*"

These particular scriptures emphasize the sovereign purpose of God in the distribution and operation of spiritual gifts.

If the preoccupation with speaking in tongues can be escaped or at least recognized as the straitjacket that it is, the result can be the experiencing of genuine gifts of the Holy Spirit on a wide scale with a minimum of demonic deception. A more mature understanding of spiritual gifts is certain to result. Along with that maturity will come a recognition that the gifts themselves are not marks of spirituality and were never intended so to be.

Another result would certainly be a further and fuller equipping of Christ's body, the church, so that it might function effectively.

There are encouraging signs, too.

According to one writer, many of the young people in the "Jesus generation" have experienced spiritual gifts after true conversion to Christ. And they have sometimes spoken in tongues. But they have been so hooked on love that in many cases they just have not wanted to insist that all must speak in tongues or even that all must have any particular spiritual gift.

Since the early nineteen hundreds there have been in North America growing holiness groups and other groups of evangelicals which have emphasized the absolute necessity of a life-changing encounter with the Holy Spirit, though not the experience of speaking in tongues. Their churches number in the thousands and their adherents in the millions. Some Baptist groups, the Church of God from Anderson, Indiana, the Nazarenes, the Christian and Missionary Alliance and the Free Methodists are but five examples.

If the "third view" of the charismata has any natural seedbed, it could be among these evangelicals. I am sure that thousands of truly charismatic (though not necessarily tongues-speaking) people are found among them.

From groups such as these, more than any others, should come the balanced view that we are calling here the "gentle maybe."

There are also rumblings of change among such strong Pentecostal bodies as the Assemblies of God. Whether they ever will retreat from their insistence that all believers speak in tongues is questionable, but I believe there is a minority among them that believes that only some will speak in tongues.

David Wilkerson, probably America's best-known Pentecostal minister, has some amazing things to say. I say *amazing* because he is a Pentecostal spokesman, though he does not claim to speak for the Assemblies of God.

> I speak with tongues in my secret closet of prayer. It is a beautiful devotional experience with me. It is not a group or public experience. No one else involved but Jesus and Me! And when a brother in Christ comes to me and says, "I believe I too have a wonderful Holy Ghost baptism, and I've never spoken in tongues," I say, "Praise God—I believe you." Why should there be any argument? We should rejoice in each other's love for Christ. . . .
>
> Those who speak with tongues must put the fruits of the Spirit above the gift. A truly baptized Christian will not drink, smoke, curse, or indulge in anything unholy or unChristlike. He must not consider the gift of tongues as a cure-all, end-it-all, best-of-all, experience. It is just a starting place. There is so much more. If a person who speaks with tongues honestly believes God is controlling his speech—when he comes back down to earth and speaks with his understanding, he had better not gossip, back bite or verbally assassinate another brother. Tongues should be a Holy Ghost mouthwash."
>
> . . . Away with thinking that everybody who speaks with tongues is a saint. Away with trying to force it on others who do not seek it.[1]

Again, the Pentecostalism developing among Roman Catholics is especially interesting because of two important facts. First, there is explosive numerical growth among the charismatic Roman Catholics. The twenty-two thousand Catholics who attended the seventh annual Catholic Charismatic Renewal Movement at Notre Dame, South Bend, Indiana, in 1973, were more than twice as numerous as the conference guests the year before. Growth of Pentecostalism within the Roman Catholic Church cannot be described in terms of addition. It is multiplication. (Statistics for 1974 enforce this view.)

Edward E. Plowman, reporting for *Christianity Today*, filed this account:

> Call it spiritual renewal, revival, or whatever, something big and evangelically beautiful is happening in the Roman Catholic Church. Tens of thousands of Catholics around the world are saying they are studying Scriptures on a scope unprecedented in Catholic history. They are the fastest growing and most important movement in Catholicism today. If the movement continues to grow at the same rate it has shown in its first six years, within a decade the majority of America's Catholics will be part of it. It is mushrooming even faster in some places abroad.[2]

Secondly, and pertinent to this chapter, Plowman makes a further observation:

> Moreover, Catholic Pentecostal doctrine distresses the classical Pentecostalists who spawned the movement. The latter believe that glossolalia is the necessary, universal sign of Spirit baptism. The Catholic charismatics reject this position, believing instead that tongues is only one of many spiritual gifts. What then is the evidence of baptism? "A transformed life— the fruit of the Spirit," replied leader Stephen Clark in a press conference.[3]

What will happen ultimately? No one really

knows of course, but a renewal appears to be taking place in Roman Catholicism, and the form seems to be charismatic. Even those who disagree with the theology of what is happening must rejoice that the Catholics in large numbers are finding Christ, reading the Bible—and perhaps speaking in tongues.

The implications are incalculable. If the dominant charismatic force ultimately resides within Roman Catholicism and at the same time avoids the fixation with tongues that has locked contemporary Pentecostalism into a rigid position, the charismatic of the future may adopt something similar to what we are calling the "third view."

Jamie Buckingham, writing in the charismatic *Logos Journal*, has a very interesting comment.

> Although the charismatic renewal of today contains many of the features of classic Pentecostalism, it is not to be confused with the old line Pentecostal denominations. "Speaking in tongues" has almost become synonymous with the move because it is usually the first outward manifestation of the inner work of the spirit. However, while traditional Pentecostals hold that tongues is "the evidence" of the baptism in the Holy Spirit (going as far as to state that unless one speaks in tongues he has not received the Holy Spirit), most charismatics feel that the "evidence" of the baptism is inner power and the ability to witness for Jesus Christ. Tongues, while accepted as a valuable and desirable part of the normal walk in the Spirit, is generally understood to be a prayer language, given for direct communication with God.[4]

It appears that the burgeoning charismatic movement, from Buckingham's view at least, is retreating from the open insistence that all must speak in tongues.

If the charismatic movement ultimately moves on to more scriptural ground, the wholesale demonic penetration of it is certain to be greatly reduced.

As I have already indicated, a large number of Christians already incline to what I am calling here the "gentle maybe." Some speak in tongues and some do not. The young people, the holiness groups, the evangelicals who emphasize the fullness of the Holy Spirit, the Roman Catholic charismatics, some within the charismatic movement, and a minority within the staunch Pentecostal denominations—all find common ground here.

The ultimate result could be balance, spiritual health, and a new atmosphere of love. Certainly Satan will be fighting hard to hinder, but I foresee a new era of the Holy Spirit where Christ is first, where the spiritual gifts are recognized for what they are—and no more—and where the tongues controversy is finally shunted aside.

Perhaps David Wilkerson says it best:

> I am praying for a new day, a day of real love when we can say, "In Christ, we are one." A day where the upper room does not overshadow the cross. A day when we can lay aside our doctrinal differences and see the Christ in one another. A day in which we no longer call ourselves by some denominational tag, but we call ourselves simply—The Jesus People! A day when we put aside all controversy and begin "in honor preferring one another." A day when we will no longer get hung up on tongues, or modes of water baptism, or manners of sanctification, or measures of grace. But instead work

> together to save a lost world while it is day.
> Lord, let there be love! [5]

Among some of God's children today there needs to be a new atmosphere of trust—where the genuine manifestations of the Holy Spirit are allowed and encouraged, where discerning mature leaders are able to guide hungry hearted believers into a wholesome experience of the spiritual gifts.

Among other of God's children today there needs to be a new willingness to question, to discern, to judge, to try the spirits—where the genuine manifestations of the Holy Spirit are allowed and encouraged, but where fleshly and demonic manifestations are uncompromisingly excised from the body of Christ.

For some of us it is a step to the right. For others of us it is a step to the left. But should we hesitate longer to move to the safety of biblical ground? I think not.

The world is lost. Men and women are going to hell. As author Pete Gillquist says, "Let's Quit Fighting About the Holy Spirit." The enemy is the devil, not your brother.

Now I will admit that what I have said about the "Gentle Maybe" is optimistic. It expresses my hopes. But I must be realistic. I confess to some second thoughts. Historically, the church has not often been ready to respond to corrective currents. The "Gentle Maybe" could be useless utopian thinking, hopeless idealism. It may never happen. But something else could happen.

So permit me please, a paragraph of pessimism. I have accented the positive so I will postscript the negative. The charismatic movement shows uncomfortable tendencies toward ecumenicalism. The churches today which seek unity at all costs are finding that they cannot unite on the basis of doctrine and theology. But the fact that Pentecostals, modernists, and Roman Catholics who have received "the baptism" can pray together and "feel" great unity is not lost on the ecumenicalists. There is a strong possibility that the ecumenicalism of the future will be based on the charismatic experience. And it will not matter if a man is saved or lost, if a man believes in the virgin birth or not, nor if he prays to God through Mary or the Lord Jesus Christ. All that will matter will be the "baptism of the Spirit." I say we forget at our peril that the false prophets Jesus warned against had charismatic abilities. The superchurch of the last days may be ecumenical, charismatic—and false.

CHAPTER 20

How to Receive Spiritual Gifts

May I begin by saying that as a Christian I have had a satisfying, delightful experience through the years in the gifts of the Spirit. From nearly the very first I have realized that the manifestations of the Holy Spirit did not make me spiritual, but they could certainly prove to be channels of God's power.

I knew enough about the gifts of the Holy Spirit to expect that when He filled me with the Holy Spirit for the first time, some gift would sooner or later be manifested. And I certainly was not disappointed.

Over the years I have realized a need in my life and ministry for certain gifts. After submitting to our Lord who divides severally as He wills, I have on a number of occasions coveted earnestly and actually received spiritual gifts which then began to function effectively. In each case there was a definite time and place in God's loving plan for my life for the manifestation of spiritual gifts. On one occasion a very useful and supernatural gift came without even asking or coveting. All praise to the Lord.

Gifts are for believers, of course. I see little biblical warrant for believing that anyone apart from bona-fide Christians might receive gifts of the Holy Spirit. And all Paul's comments on the matter are set in a church context.

Spiritual gifts may be expected to follow the initial infilling of the Holy Spirit. This is a biblical pattern that holds true today. There may be a time lapse between the filling of the Spirit and the manifestation of the spiritual gift God has chosen to give. It is important to remember that the Bible stops short of showing by example that all who are filled with the Holy Spirit will speak in tongues, and it also makes it clear, "Do all speak with tongues?" "No."

Spiritual gifts may also come into the life of a believer through the laying on of hands and prophecy. Many Christian groups set apart young men for the ministry with the laying on of hands. And it is a most appropriate time to believe God for spiritual gifts, as He wills.

Paul's experience with Timothy was followed by this exhortation: "Neglect not the gift that is in thee, which was given thee by prophecy, with the laying on of the hands of the presbytery" (1 Tim. 4:14).

Evidently there had been prophecy and the reception of a spiritual gift when Timothy was set apart for God's work.

In this present time, one group known to me in the United States apparently has a balanced practice of the spiritual gifts which often function when hands are publicly laid upon the missionaries to be sent out to the fields of the world.

I could certainly sense, as one of their leaders related this to me, just how deeply moved and touched he had been by prophecy, given with the laying on of hands.

I want to make clear that such a wonderful experience is not limited to His ministering servants. All of God's children may receive spiritual gifts, "The manifestation of the Spirit is given to every man to profit withal."

And that brings us to another concept. Spiritual gifts engender spiritual gifts. They are divisible, something like the widow's oil in Elijah's time. And if you will pardon the negative connotation—spiritual gifts are contagious.

Spiritual gifts may come into the life through contact with and the sharing of another brother. "As every man hath received the gift, even so minister the same one to another, as good stewards of the manifold grace of God" (1 Pet. 4:10).

The significance of the laying on of hands can be underestimated at this point. (See Appendix B.)

Also, when certain spiritual gifts are functioning, they are the ones which will be communicated to others, in the will of God. For example, there may be a flow of gifts of healings in one group of God's children, of prophecy in another, and tongues in yet another. Many but not all of those in each group will receive the dominant gift, while lesser numbers will receive other gifts. We are assuming Christ-adorning behavior and constant submission to the will of God in all of this.

A word of warning here: a person should not lightly submit to the laying on of hands. If there is any reason at all to be concerned that the spiritual operations are carnal, false, or even demonic, stay away. A fair percentage of Christians under occult bondage and even victims of demon invasion have gotten into that bondage through allowing unholy hands to be laid upon them.

This warning, though, is not intended to stop anyone from coveting earnestly in the will of God any true spiritual gift. The banquet table is loaded with goodness. There will be no problems to those who stay on biblical ground. But once off biblical ground, Jesus' blood does not cover you.

Satan must not, by deceptions and false gifts, divert the church from the reality which exists. A counterfeit five dollar bill would never exist were it not that the genuine exists also. Society never discards the money system because of the counterfeits. Instead, it deals with the counterfeiters and then proceeds with the business of the nation.

For too long the church of Jesus Christ has been saying, "It's all counterfeit," or, "There's no such thing as money," or, "There's no such thing as counterfeit." Isn't it time to be truly discerning, to get on with God's business? And in this context that business is to follow after love and desire spiritual gifts.

The gifts of the Spirit come in answer to prayer and faith. "What things soever ye desire, when ye pray, believe that ye receive them, and ye shall have them" (Mark 11:24).

Desire spiritual gifts. Covet earnestly the best gifts. Do not forget the more excellent way. This is God's plan for the experiencing of the spiritual gifts.

When a new manifestation of the Holy Spirit comes into your life, the best advice is to hold your peace and give yourself six months or a year to cope with the initial excitement of a wholly new spiritual operation.

Make yourself remember that gifts are not marks of spirituality; instead, they are new indications of usefulness to Christ. Dead trees can carry gifts in their branches, but only live trees can bear fruit. Remember too that spiritual gifts are weapons, tools, to do the work of Christ.

Finally, love is more powerful, more effective, and more important than all of these gifts. If God had said that we must choose love *or* gifts, our choice would beyond question be love.

However, God does not say that. Instead He says, "Follow after charity, and desire spiritual gifts, but rather that ye may prophesy" (1 Cor. 14:1).

CHAPTER 21

So What Do You Do?

How do you write a book about tongues when you do not know the experience yourself? More importantly, when the main thrust of your book, not to mention the Scriptures, makes it clear that the gifts are divided severally as God wills, what do you do?

And if you are not especially anxious to speak in tongues, what do you do?

And if you know very well that God filled you with the Holy Spirit years ago and that for years you have had a satisfying experience in the spiritual gifts without speaking in tongues, what do you do?

If you know your more enthusiastic charismatic brethren will probably refuse all you say because you do not speak in tongues, what do you do?

And if you do speak in tongues you know that some will say, "Now he has the baptism," when really you know in your heart that even if you do speak in tongues, that is not what will have happened at all. What do you do?

And if you know that speaking in tongues can give your book an authority and impact it would not otherwise have, what do you do?

And if you realize that your motive for wanting to speak in tongues may be just to add effectiveness to a book, rather than desiring a beautiful gift of the Holy Spirit for God's glory, what do you do?

You pray.

So I prayed. Something like this: "Lord, if you would like to allow me in your will to speak in tongues, I'm willing for whatever you have for me. I submit myself unconditionally to your will. I make no demands. I refuse and reject everything that is of the devil and I welcome all that is of the Holy Spirit of Almighty God."

And so it was that during the writing of this book the Lord answered my prayer by giving me the manifestation of tongues.

At this point I could take the "experience book route" and provide all the details about providential circumstances, feelings, etc. But I feel restrained at the same time. Perhaps the reason is that there is no biblical basis for describing the subjective details relating to an experience with any of the gifts of the Holy Spirit. Though I will admit these same details are often fascinating and exciting.

I will say that I immediately made sure that the manifestation was one that willingly confessed that Jesus Christ is come in the flesh. And frankly, though the Scriptures do not require that wariness in every case, in this age of charismatic confusion I personally could never rest unless I knew the source of such a manifestation in my life and ministry.

I'm not suggesting the same experience for you. Certainly not all speak with tongues.

God is not at all impoverished in His methods. He does not even duplicate a snowflake exactly. But our Lord still divides severally as He wills, thank God.

When I told my wife on the phone what had happened, she wondered how I could be so subdued about it all. My reply was spontaneous—and revealing. I said impulsively, "It would be hard to handle if you were (initially) filled with the Holy Spirit at the same time." That is it exactly. It also would be harder to handle if you thought it was a necessity, or the only evidence of being filled with the Holy Spirit. Or if you had no previous experience with the function of other spiritual gifts.

I suppose I am a reluctant arrival among the tongues-speakers. But I believe God wants this witness. Really, there should be no need at all to divulge the secrets of our hearts. Still, I have felt that if I wanted to really help people, I would have to speak up. Confusion and deception must not go on forever. And because the church of our Lord is hurting, wounded and bleeding, thrust through with "tongues," I have no choice but to add my witness.

Not that it is unbiblical to do so. There is a scriptural precedent. In the midst of all his corrective writings to the Corinthians Paul said, "I speak with tongues more than you all." He talked from his experience when it became necessary. Paul is the only biblical writer to claim a spiritual gift publicly, and he did so in a corrective context.

Though I certainly am not presuming any Pauline authority, this "third view" could be corrective. I want it to be that. It is personal. And for good or ill, it has become in its own way an experience book too. If it finds its place alongside the other experience books as a counterweight and a balance, it will be more than I can ask.

Epilogue

This has been a fascinating book to write because I have found that many other people have had important contributions to make. Though I have not provided any footnotes for these helpful comments, I wish to thank all who have reviewed the manuscript. Regardless of their views, they have invariably helped me.

This book is an international one. The first draft came in the Dominican Republic. Revisions were made in charismatic Chile. Further revisions continued in Gabon and Canada. The message was completed in Boma, Republic of Zaire. So it has not been written in a corner. The phenomena about which I have written are similar everywhere.

My final efforts have been to polish it and to wrap more love into it. Now I send it forth with prayer. May our Lord, the Great Shepherd of so many sheep in so many lands, use it as He sees fit.

Can a Christian Be Controlled by Demons?

These words may not be necessary. Traditionally, many evangelicals have stoutly held that no Christian can ever come under the influence of demons. Almost invariably those who insisted on this had never actually been involved in exorcisms. But with the occult invasion of North America an obvious fact, more and more Christian leaders are being involved in deliverances. And they are finding that sincere Christian believers can and do come under demonic power. Experience, if nothing else, is forcing evangelicals to take a second look.

Merril F. Unger, in his classic work, *Biblical Demonology*, took the position that no Christian could ever be controlled by demons. Evidently in response to reactions from Christian workers around the world, Mr. Unger has revised his position in a more recent book entitled *Demons in the World Today*.

The late V. Raymond Edman, once Chancellor of Wheaton College, firmly believed that Christians could be controlled by demons, though not to the same degree as the unconverted. Citing the tripartite view of man, Edman believed that demonic influence could be exerted in the bodily and soulish areas of Christians. He inclined to believe that the spirit of the Christian remained invulnerable to demons. Personally, I favor his view. And in numerous experiences with exorcism over the years, I recall only one case where an unconverted person was involved. All other cases were Christians in trouble.

Scripture, of course, is the final court of appeal. It is significant to me that Paul spoke of the possibility of receiving "another spirit" (2 Cor. 11:4). Though the Corinthians had not received such a spirit, this comment was made to a church which dealt with demonic disease (Matt. 4:24), and there is no suggestion anywhere in the Bible that there are some diseases Christians cannot get.

Christian believers do not need to go around ducking demons and cowering with fear. But they need to be careful. If Satan is given ground, he takes it. And he does so regardless of the theological niceties.

The Laying On of Hands

Hebrews 6:1, 2 clearly indicates that the laying on of hands is one of the principles of the doctrine of Christ. It is a principle that every new convert should understand and from which he should go on.

"Therefore let us go on and get past the elementary stage in the teachings and doctrine of Christ, the Messiah, advancing steadily toward the completeness and perfection that belongs to spiritual maturity. Let us not again be laying the foundation of repentance and abandonment of dead works [dead formalism], and of the faith [by which you turned] to God.

"With teachings about purifying, the laying on of hands, the resurrection from the dead, and eternal judgment and punishment. [These are all matters of which you should have been fully aware long, long ago]" (Heb. 6:1, 2, The Amplified New Testament).

Many times, however, there is great ignorance on this principle. And Christians are not aware of the tremendous significance of the laying on of hands.

In the Word, a number of uses are found for the laying on of hands:

1. In identification with a sacrifice as an offering for sin (Lev. 1:4, 3:2, 3:8, 3:13, 4:4, 4:15).

2. In putting sin upon the scapegoat or bullock (Lev. 16:21). There is a very interesting passage in Numbers 8:10-12.

3. In witnessing an accusation (Lev. 24:14).

4. In imparting the Holy Spirit (Num. 27:18-23, Deut. 34:9, Acts 8:17, 9:12, 19:16).

5. In imparting blessing (Gen. 48:13-15, Matt. 19:15, Mark 10:16).

6. In healing the sick (Mark 1:41, 6:5, 16:18).

7. In imparting spiritual gifts (1 Tim. 4:14).

8. In working special miracles through Paul's hands (Acts 19:11).

9. In ordaining elders. In Acts 14:23 the word "ordain" means to stretch forth the hand.

May I insert a word of warning: "Lay hands suddenly on no man" (1 Tim. 5:22).

This ministry of laying on of hands can be of great assistance to the believer who desires effectiveness. While some of the usages are clearly for Old Testament times only, several of these usages have a definite New Testament application.

Notes

NOTES TO CHAPTER 2

1. Merrill F. Unger, *New Testament Teaching on Tongues* (Grand Rapids, Michigan: Kregel Publications, 1971), pp. 28-33, 91-98. Used with permission.

2. Dennis and Rita Bennett, *The Holy Spirit and You* (Plainfield, New Jersey: Logos International, 1971), pp. 64-65, 70, 75, 81, 89. Used with permission.

NOTES TO CHAPTER 3

1. Pat Boone, *A New Song* (Carol Stream, Illinois: Creation House, 1970), p. 127.

2. John L. Sherrill, *They Speak with Other Tongues* (Old Tappan, New Jersey: Fleming H. Revell Company, 1964:), p. 83. Used with permission.

3. Sherrill, *loc. cit.*, pp. 122-123. Used with permission.

4. Frances Gardner Hunter, *The Two Sides of a Coin* (Van Nuys, California: Spire Books, 1972), p. 53.

NOTES TO CHAPTER 4

1. Larry Christenson, *Speaking in Tongues* (Minneapolis, Minnesota: Bethany Fellowship, Inc., 1968), p. 54. Used with permission.
2. K. Neill Foster, *Six Conditions for the Filling of the Holy Spirit* (Kamloops, British Columbia: by the author, n.d.), p. 12.

NOTES TO CHAPTER 6

1. T. H. McCrossan, *Speaking With Other Tongues* (Harrisburg, Pa.: Christian Publications, Inc., n.d.).
2. Don Basham, *True & False Prophets* (Greensburg, Pa.: Manna Books, 1973), pp. 40-41. Used with permission.

NOTES TO CHAPTER 9

1. Siegfried Crossman, *There Are Other Gifts Than Tongues* (Wheaton, Illinois: Key Publishers, Inc., 1971), p. 111. Used with permission.

NOTES TO CHAPTER 11

1. Raymond McFarlane Kincheloe, *A Study of Spiritual Gifts* (Regina, Saskatchewan: unpublished paper), p. 3. Used with permission.
2. Larry Christenson, *Speaking in Tongues* (Minneapolis, Minnesota: Bethany Fellowship, Inc., 1968), p. 121. Used with permission.

NOTES TO CHAPTER 13

1. Gerald E. McGraw, *Alliance Witness* (New York, N.Y.: June 5, 1974), p. 3.

2. Kevin and Dorothy Ranaghan, *Catholic Pentecostals* (Paramus, New Jersey: Paulist Press, 1969), p. 70.

NOTES TO CHAPTER 18

1. Jessie Penn-Lewis, *War on the Saints* (Fort Washington, Pa.: Christian Literature Crusade, n.d.), p. 8.

NOTES TO CHAPTER 19

1. David Wilkerson, *David Wilkerson Speaks Out* (Minneapolis, Minnesota: Bethany Fellowship, Inc., 1973), pp. 17, 19, 20. Used with permission.
2. Edward E. Plowman, *Christianity Today* (Washington, D.C., June 22, 1973), p. 36. Used with permission.
3. *Ibid.*, p. 37. Used with permission.
4. Jamie Buckingham, *Logos Journal* (Plainfield, New Jersey, September-October 1973), p. 8. Used with permission.
5. Wilkerson, *loc. cit.*, p. 21-22. Used with permission.